The Pre-Raphaelite Trail In Dorset:
An Arts and Crafts Tour

Peter Wise

S.B. Publications

DEDICATION
For my mother, Jessie.

First published in 2013 by S. B. Publications

For further copies of this book please contact:
peterrwise@yahoo.com
sbpublications@tiscali.co.uk

ISBN 978-1-85770-370-2

Designed and Typeset by EH Graphics, East Sussex Tel: 07734 923 796
Email: elizhowe515527@gmail.com

FRONT COVER: (clockwise from upper left)
"VENUS VERTICORDIA" BY DANTE GABRIEL ROSSETTI. PERMISSION OF RUSSELL-COTES ART GALLERY AND MUSEUM.
MINTERNE GARDENS.
DETAIL OF ST. CATHERINE WINDOW BY ROBERT ANNING BELL IN ABBOTSBURY CHURCH.
STOURPAINE CHURCH AND LYCHGATE.

TITLE PAGE: *COLEHILL CHURCH*

BACK COVER: *CHRISTOPHER WHALL WINDOW AT WEST STAFFORD*

Contents

DETAIL OF MARY LOWNDES STAINED GLASS AT STURMINSTER NEWTON

The Author

Peter Wise is an art historian with a particular interest in Victorian and Edwardian fine art and design. He has written two previous books The Pre-Raphaelite Trail in Sussex (2003, revised 2008) and The Pre-Raphaelite Trail in Kent (2009). He is a member of the William Morris Society, the Pre-Raphaelite Society and the Kempe Society. He currently resides in Ilfracombe, North Devon with his family.

The author is most grateful to the many scholars, rectors, vicars, church wardens and other individuals who provided invaluable help and assistance with this book.

The author has checked the information contained in this book and believes it to be correct, and cleared copyright if appropriate. If however, there is an unforeseen infringement in copyright the author apologises for this.

The author encourages comments about this book from readers, in particular any new information about the subjects discussed. E-mail address: peterrwise@yahoo.com

Preface

The Pre-Raphaelite painters created a uniquely British revolution in the art world of their time. They did this by challenging the established academic practice of the day, seeking different subjects to portray and painting these with the most astonishing attention to detail. Their pictures might show a contemporary story or depict a scene from medieval times, but invariably the countryside they painted was entirely naturalistic. The architects and craftsmen that followed them also started a revolution seen through their buildings and artefacts, both of which were characterised by their organic form and uniqueness of design.

This book can be your companion and guide as you travel around the delightful county of Dorset discovering its Arts and Crafts architecture and following in the footsteps of Pre-Raphaelite artists, for whom its wonderful landscapes were a perpetual source of inspiration. It allows the reader to choose their own particular route based upon their personal areas of interest. You can do a full day's exploration or just a leisurely afternoon drive. The destination may be a church or art gallery or perhaps a gentle walk through a typical Dorset village. It might entail a visit to a country house open to the public or a stroll along the dramatic coastline. Alternatively, the reader need never leave their comfortable armchair to experience some of the artistic highlights of the area.

This book is a companion to two earlier volumes by the author covering the nearby counties of Kent and Sussex but can be used entirely independently.

GRAVESTONE INSCRIPTIONS BY ERIC GILL AT CRANBORNE

How to use this book

This book is mainly in the form of a gazetteer made in alphabetical order.

At the beginning of each entry are some broad directions in order to locate the village or town mentioned but these are intended as a guide only and do not take the place of a good Ordnance Survey map of the area. The Philip's and OS street atlas for Dorset provides all the required information in one slim volume. At the end of each entry is brief advice about access, including visiting times for buildings and properties open to the public. A large number of the churches listed are unlocked during daylight hours, but it is always a good idea to have a mobile phone with you so that you can call a church warden if there are any difficulties seeing the interior of a building. Their contact details are usually to be found on the sign for the church or on the noticeboard often located in the porch. In the text of each entry important artists, architects or craftspeople are highlighted in bold lettering which refers to a name in the biographical index. There are also artists in the index whose work is in the Russell-Cotes Art Gallery collection.

DETAIL OF KEMPE & CO. GLASS AT WEST LULWORTH

Introduction

Now more popular than ever and even the subject of a recent bawdy television romp the Pre-Raphaelite Brotherhood was initially very much a secret society. Its central motivation was to destabilise the Establishment and to this purpose its members formulated a set of ideals that all those involved believed in and would abide by.

Although the members of the Brotherhood were young artists and their particular grievance was with the conservative art world of the late eighteen-forties, it was also a time of real rebellion. Europe was engulfed by wars with many countries in states of turmoil. In this atmosphere of uncertainty and change, it is perhaps not so surprising that three men barely (or not quite) in their twenties had the idea to form a revolutionary group. The three principal protagonists were Dante Gabriel Rossetti, John Everett Millais and William Holman Hunt.

Much has been written about the private lives of these three painters who together with four other prospective artists made up the Brotherhood. Millais was the subject of a major scandal when he met and fell in love with Effie Ruskin, who of course later divorced her husband and married him. Rossetti's claim to the infamous must be the disinterment of his beloved Lizzie Siddal's grave in order to retrieve his poems rashly buried with her so he could latterly publish them. Even Holman Hunt is not immune from fallout in lieu of his close relationship with a likely prostitute Annie Miller and his misguided attempts to refine her.

But for the time being, let's focus more on their artistic pursuits and how they chose to subvert the old practices of the day and contravene the rules associated with these, in order to produce a new and startling form of painting. One that was based (at least in the early years) on reproducing what they saw in the world to a new level of high detail and with astonishing brightness. As a means of doing this, the members of the Brotherhood and their followers took the then radical step of leaving their studios and painting directly in front of their chosen subject usually, without reference to whatever the weather could do to make this process problematic. This novel approach to art was influenced by a number of new developments then prevalent in society. One of the main strides forward was the advent of photography but there were also advances in the understanding of geology and in natural history and these are reflected in the subject matter of many Pre-Raphaelite paintings. Even those artists more interested in showing contemporary subject matter or historical scenes in preference to landscape would have a very detailed background to the main story of the painting thus making every aspect of the picture as important as another.

It's true that the original members of the Brotherhood have few documented connections to Dorset although fellow painter John Brett did visit the county on at least three occasions (see separate chapter) as did Walter Crane a leading figure not just in painting but also politically advocating the importance of a return to pre-Industrial values. However, the Pre-Raphaelite influence can be felt from one end of the county to the other. This is particularly evident in the stained glass windows of Morris & Co.

whose chief designer was Edward Burne-Jones. Both William Morris and Burne-Jones were major artist-designers associated with the second wave of the Pre-Raphaelites that is to say, younger men who had come under the spell of the original Brotherhood that to all intents and purposes had come to an end by 1855. Morris in particular, challenged the Victorian proliferation of shoddy goods produced in factories as they had been from the start of the Industrial Revolution and instead wanted artists and designers to make thoughtful and beautiful things in the fields of architecture, furniture, metalwork and furnishings amongst others. He was convinced that the quality of design and craftsmanship reflected on the moral goodness of the world around them. One of the most obvious aspects of these new pieces of work was their reliance on a naturalistic depiction of nature where little is exaggerated just for effect. This work was to be produced using traditional skills acquired through increased opportunities in training and education and with reference to the past. It was felt that this in turn would enhance people's lives (both workers and customers) and therefore create a more just and civilised society.

Rossetti and other artists such as Ford Madox-Brown turned to designing items such as stained glass windows or furniture for Morris's firm in addition to painting. A movement for change began to be established in many of the cities and there was also a move to have craft communities in more rural areas. The Art Workers' Guild was founded in 1884. Women began to be involved in the various Art and Crafts guilds and societies (as they came to be called after 1888) that were set up and this coincided with a time of greater equality for women (although there was a considerable way to go-many of the female designers were also involved with the suffragette cause).

In addition a greater closeness developed between the arts and crafts and manufacturing and this can be gauged by the better links forged by people such as Christopher Dresser and W.A.S. Benson who wanted design reform but thought it could be achieved by using mechanical means. Here style was given more priority and there was less emphasis on the importance of the process of making an object.

Men such as C.F.A. Voysey were part of a later generation to embrace the ideals of the Art and Crafts movement- an artist as well as an architect who used these skills in his design plans drawing from nature and then designing buildings using these motifs. His way of working owed much to A.W.N. Pugin who was a great inspiration to the new Art and Crafts practitioners many of whom wished also to celebrate the Gothic style as he had done. The importance of this style was discussed by John Ruskin and many examples of Gothic Revival buildings appear in this book because they were an integral part of the emerging movement. Morris however could be critical of the heavy architecture sometimes associated with the Victorian version of Gothic and this led him to consider freer interpretations of medieval buildings.

Dorset is lucky in having a wealth of churches of the late nineteenth and early twentieth century where it is possible to see at first hand architecture and artefacts associated with the developing Arts and Crafts movement. There are fine examples of work by celebrated practitioners but also wood and stone carving and painting by little known local artisans responding to the spirit of the time.

Although some of the Pre-Raphaelite artists involved moved on to paint entirely different works including portraiture, many continued to work mainly in landscape even if the finish was broader than when they were younger with greater reserves of energy. A particularly important resource for exploring this change in the subject matter and style pursued by painters is the Russell-Cotes Museum and Art Gallery in Bournemouth. Although the county is not the first one to come to mind as a location for considering the work of either the Pre-Raphaelite artists or the Arts and Crafts movement there are in fact a surprising number of historical threads to them. It is also quite refreshing to find such a rich collection of work in a county rarely mentioned in literature on the subject.

The Dorset County Arts and Crafts Association was formed only in 1907 but its first official exhibition was held in the imposing setting of Blandford Forum's Corn Exchange and today the Association is a rare survivor and still holds an annual exhibition.

DETAIL OF MORRIS & CO GLASS IN MARNHULL CHURCH

"THE BRITISH CHANNEL AS SEEN FROM THE DORSETSHIRE CLIFFS" BY JOHN BRETT PERMISSION OF TATE

A Pre-Raphaelite Mariner

JOHN BRETT (1831-1902)

John Brett was born in Reigate and as a boy was drawn towards two competing interests in his life-painting and astronomy. When he eventually opted for the former as a career not surprisingly it was with a scientific spirit.

From 1851 he had lessons from J.D. Harding who was primarily a landscape artist as well as tuition in drawing from another established artist of the day Richard Redgrave. He entered the Royal Academy two years later where he would have seen work by the Pre-Raphaelite Brotherhood and other artists of their circle.

In the autumn of 1853 he met William Holman Hunt at the home of the poet Coventry Patmore. Brett was also friendly with Millais and Rossetti at this period of time. He read the books of Ruskin (in particular Modern Painters IV) and these influences inspired Brett to go to Switzerland in June 1856 where he produced the stunning *The Glacier at Rosenlaui*. This picture shows the glacier in scrupulous detail and the rocks surrounding it have a geological emphasis. The work was highly regarded by Ruskin and enthused by his praise Brett completed two further works soon after now regarded as amongst his most important paintings namely *The Stonebreaker* and *Val d'Aosta*. Both pictures are characterised by a Pre-Raphaelite attention to naturalistic detail.

"CHRISTMAS MORNING, 1866" BY JOHN BRETT
PERMISSION OF RUSSELL-COTES ART GALLERY AND MUSEUM.

After staying in Florence in 1861-2 he sailed around the Mediterranean the year later and it is from this time that he starts to concentrate on coastal scenes and seascapes. An early example of these is *Christmas Morning, 1866* completed in 1868 and now in the Russell-Cotes Art Gallery and Museum.

It was not until 1870 however, that Brett took an extensive tour around the south-west coast of England which he did in the company of Mary Ann Howcroft who he had met the previous year and with whom he was to have seven children. He made a series of small water-colours during the trip which he later used in his studio as the basis for much larger oils. One of these was *The British Channel seen from the Dorsetshire Cliffs* (see illustration) which shows a spectacularly wide view of the sea lit by shafts of sunlight and observed from a high vantage point that was probably near Lulworth Cove. The picture emphasises the vastness of the expanse by depicting tiny sailing boats upon the sea. This wonderful work caused quite a stir when it was exhibited at the Pre-Raphaelite Vision exhibition at the Tate in 2004 mainly because it was relatively unknown having been stored out of sight for many years. On the same tour Brett completed a number of watercolours and sketches of the Lulworth area at differing times of day and in a variety of weather. He also worked at nearby Oswald Bay, around Purbeck and Portland and at Durdle Door. Other titles he worked on include *From Durlstone Head Dorset, Peveril Point, Sunset effect off Charmouth Dorset, Sunset off Lyme coasts* and several water-colour studies of Swanage at varying times of the day.

Based on a sketch made at this time Brett produced the oil called *Man of War Rocks, Dorset* in 1884 for his patron Dr. James Watt Black which provided much needed finance for another trip down the Dorset coast in the summer of that year.

By this time Brett had bought a two hundred and ten ton schooner which he named the Viking. This cost him over a thousand pounds and necessitated paying twelve men to be the yacht's crew. With his wife and children on board, a cruise could be an anxiety provoking experience particularly in bad weather but the boat could also be used for socialising and the guests on these occasions included the fellow marine artist Henry Moore and the Scottish water-colourist Francis Powell.

When Brett and his family were anchored at Portland they were close to the Channel fleet and they had contact with the officers of HMS Northumberland and Brett made sketches of the ship and the surrounding area including Whitenose and Chesil Beach.

The last year that Brett produced a significant amount of work was 1897 and this was when he once again passed through Dorset en route to Cornwall. This was not on board the Viking which he had not used since 1885. Certainly, the schooner had been expensive to run and in the later years of his career Brett found himself increasingly starved of income especially as he had such a large family to support. He seems to have again favoured Swanage as a location for sketching later completing the painting *A Squally Day at Swanage* which was shown at the Royal Academy in 1901 shortly before his death in January of the following year aged seventy. Mary was to outlive him by nine years.

Although it is true to say that John Brett spent more time painting in Cornwall and Wales it would appear that the coastline of Dorset provided him with much inspiration throughout his life.

A Mansion of Art

THE RUSSELL-COTES ART GALLERY AND MUSEUM

This intriguing building houses an astonishing collection of mainly Victorian art and sculpture collected by Merton Russell-Cotes and Annie Nelson Clark.

Merton hailed from Tettenhall near Wolverhampton but spent much of his childhood in Glasgow where he was brought up by his mother, sister and brother-in-law following the death of his father when Merton was only seven years of age. Whilst in the city he met John King Clark whose father was a big cotton spinner and the two became close friends. Later Merton met Clark's daughter Annie and despite spending a number of years in Buenos Aires for health reasons he married her in Glasgow when he returned there in 1860. The couple then settled in Dublin where they had five children although two died young. Merton was prone to illness in particular bronchitis and on doctor's orders moved to the south coast of England as it was considered that this warmer climate may be beneficial to his health. Merton and Annie with their family eventually decided to move permanently to Bournemouth and ensconced themselves in the Bath Hotel on the resort's seafront. They began to appreciate the charms of the developing town a feeling enhanced by Merton's improved health.

The couple later decided to buy the hotel and to refurbish it in a more luxurious style and at the end of this work the building was reborn as the Royal Bath Hotel in 1880. Much involved in the life of the town and now financially more than secure, Merton began to collect art and sculpture in abundance initially to furnish the hotel with sophisticated artefacts that his mannered guests would appreciate. These were mainly acquired on extended overseas holidays and after a visit to Japan that they particularly enjoyed, they created a special room in the hotel devoted to the items purchased there. Merton eventually became Mayor of the town and in this position was able to prevent planned development along the promenade between the town and nearby Boscombe. This meant that his hotel was not compromised and his collecting continued unabated. The idea that his extensive collection needed a custom made place to house it then developed and Merton and Annie began to plan the building of East Cliff Hall now known as the Russell-Cotes Art Gallery and Museum.

The building was designed by a local architect by the name of John Frederick Fogerty and was constructed to the east of the hotel but within its grounds. Its design was certainly eclectic and Nikolaus Pevsner later described it as *'thoroughly debased'* by which he meant that it was not of one recognisable style. In fact it is a mix of French chateau and Scottish baronial but with added Italian characteristics. The house was completed by 1901 and Merton presented it to his wife on the occasion of her birthday. It was, and still is, a suitable but eccentric venue for the display of sumptuous fine art, decorative art and sculpture. It resembles a prosperous Victorian artist's home such as can still be seen at Leighton House in Kensington, London. Although now functioning solely as an art gallery and museum, it was originally intended to be a family house with all the important rooms facing the sea and with fine views. The most imposing space has to be the central hall then as now, full to brimming with paintings, ceramics and sculpture.

In 1908 Merton and Annie presented East Cliff Hall to the town of Bournemouth on the proviso that they could continue to live in it whilst the general public could visit on one day per week. Merton was knighted a year later in recognition of this gift and the building was extended in 1913-19 with the addition of three further art galleries.

Merton and Annie died in 1921 and 1920 respectively, and a year after the death of Merton the house was officially opened to the public. A fourth gallery was added later by the Russell-Cotes' son and daughter.

Within the interior of the house are a number of seminal Pre-Raphaelite paintings with some lesser known gems as well.

THE RUSSELL-COTES ART GALLERY AND MUSEUM

The works include:

Christmas Morning, 1866 by **John Brett** (see illustration in chapter on Brett p12)

This painting is the second largest work that the artist ever completed. It depicts the shipwreck of the steamship London that took place in the Bay of Biscay in the same year but at a different date. At the time Brett was in the habit of giving his painting enigmatic titles, which may partially explain his decision to so title this work as above. The wreck caused some shock at the time as the steamship had a number of well known passengers including Ruskin's cousin. Of one hundred and thirty-nine people on board only nineteen survived.

Before commencing the painting Brett did a large amount of research including many sketches of the sea in all its various states some of which he made during two voyages around the British Isles that he completed just prior to going into the studio. His method of work was very different to earlier observations of nature painted on the spot, instead he used his sketch-work to provide the initial stimulus for the composition and then largely painted the picture in the studio. The painting was exhibited at the Royal Academy in 1868. There are two other paintings by the same artist in the collection entitled *The Black East Wind* and *Porth Curnow* both completed in 1880.

Aurora Triumphans by **Evelyn De Morgan**

This painting perhaps more than any other, is synonymous with the collection at the Russell-Cotes museum. It depicts the myth of *Aurora* the Greek goddess of the dawn breaking free of the shackles of the night. She is often described as 'rosy fingered' and her myth provides a romantic view of the dawn. It was painted by Evelyn Pickering as the artist was known around 1886 a year before her marriage to the potter William De Morgan.

"AURORA TRIUMPHANS" BY EVELYN DE MORGAN.
PERMISSION OF RUSSELL-COTES ART GALLERY AND MUSEUM.

The picture has a confusing inscription that appears to read EBJ 1876 suggesting it was painted by Edward Burne-Jones which has not been totally explained although it could be the attempt of an unscrupulous individual to confuse a potential buyer. The altered inscription may conceal another which might read EP 1886 the year it was exhibited at the Grosvenor Gallery by the unmarried artist. It was acquired in about 1922 by Merton Russell-Cotes.

Home from Work and *The Heavenly Stair* by **Arthur Hughes**

Although neither of these paintings belong to the period of Hughes' output that was influenced by Pre-Raphaelite ideas (largely the 1850s) they do show his unswerving loyalty to subjects of a lyrical and poetic nature (*The Heavenly Stair*) and to those of a domestic kind (*Home from Work*). Now acknowledged to be a brilliant painter of children throughout his long life, Hughes' career is usually seen as being most brightest early on with his subsequent work seeming to lack inspiration in both subject and execution. However these assumptions are more recently being questioned with for example, the later work of Millais and Brett being more positively assessed.

Home from Work has a rather convoluted history originally dating from 1870-1 when it was shown at the Royal Academy. It was retouched a couple or so years later and appeared at an exhibition in Glasgow under the title *After Work.* Following this the picture suffered more profound changes with the left-hand side of the canvas being cut down and then largely replaced and another section added to the top. Little of the original painting seems to have survived and the composition was radically altered most noticeably with the removal of the child's mother-the child herself, still seems to be looking for this disappeared figure.

The picture acquired its present title in 1921 and the work was purchased by the museum in January 1932.

The Heavenly Stair was bequeathed to the museum by Merton in 1921. Once again the size of the canvas has changed in the course of its lifetime. It dates from 1887-8 when it too was exhibited at the Royal Academy. It is considered to be the first of Hughes' late religious works and also the biggest. It can of course be compared to Burne-Jones' *The Golden Stairs* which had been shown at the Grosvenor Gallery about eight years earlier (now to be seen at Tate Britain). Whether or not that painting did provide some of the inspiration for Hughes' picture is uncertain but *The Heavenly Stair* is satisfying in its depiction of ethereal angels and a far more down to earth but modern Holy Family.

Venus Verticordia by **Dante Gabriel Rossetti** (illustrated on front cover)

This oil dating from 1863/8 shows the ancient goddess of love the Latin title of the work meaning Venus, turner of hearts. The artist's choice of title derived from a belief that Venus could turn men's affections away from their rightful lovers and therefore she conforms to a femme fatale figure. However Rossetti later understood the myth to mean that Venus turned women's hearts away from infidelity towards virtue and chastity, but he did not change the title of the painting. She holds the golden apple which was awarded to her by Paris, in a contest amongst three goddesses and in return Venus promised him Helen the most beautiful woman. It is probably the artist's sole nude and the head of Venus is seen in a very confined space with roses and honeysuckle behind. The former is of course a symbol of love and the latter a more sexual symbol. The flowers are represented naturalistically.

The Annunciation by **Simeon Solomon**

This oil dating from 1894 is one of a number of paintings by the artist with the same subject-that of Mary receiving the news from the Archangel Gabriel that she is going to bear a child, Jesus Christ. The head and shoulders of the figures are shown in profile. Although Solomon was Jewish his later work often explores other denominational beliefs.

An Autumn Pastoral, The Convent Garden, The True Love, and *The Apple Harvest* by **Noel Laura Nisbet.** These four paintings were purchased to exhibit in the Morning Room.

Gentle Spring Brings her Garden Stuff to the Market by **Amy Sawyer.**

This picture is an abstract highly decorative work much in the style of G.F. Watts.

Love Betrayed by **John Roddam Spencer Stanhope.** A typical mythological work by the artist produced in the style of Burne-Jones after Italian Renaissance pictures. It depicts Cupid falling through a gap in a wooden bridge whilst his intended lover looks on nonchalantly.

King Ahab's Coveting by **Thomas Matthews Rooke.**

This small scale picture has six scenes showing the biblical tale set within a wonderful carved frame.

'If I could have that little head of hers painted on a background of pale gold' by **Eleanor Fortescue Brickdale.**

With a title taken from a poem by Robert Browning this work is a portrait in profile.

Jezebel and *The Prodigal's Return* by **John Liston Byam Shaw.**

The first painting dates from 1896 and depicts the Old Testament tale of *King Ahab's* queen (see Thomas Rooke above) who died a particularly gruesome death (she was thrown to the dogs). The picture shows her in bright sensual clothing which she is only wearing due to Russell-Cotes's intervention. When the work was first exhibited at the Royal Academy the figure was nude and caused no little controversy, so as a condition of purchase, Russell-Cotes asked for Jezebel to be draped and the artist agreed later even commenting that the painting was improved as a result.

The latter of the two works by Byam Shaw in the collection has the New Testament story set against a backdrop painted at Ludlow Castle.

An Incantation by **The Hon. John Collier.**

A later acquisition by the gallery depicting a nude femme fatale figure.

Not all these works will be on display at any one time, so it is advisable to contact the gallery before visiting if you wish to view a specific work.

There are also tiles by Maw & Co. in the porch and fireplace tiles in the study by **Carter & Co. of Poole.**

Gazetteer

ABBOTSBURY is on the B3157 about ten miles east of Weymouth.

The CHURCH OF ST NICHOLAS stands in a truly beautiful setting with the ruins of the earlier Benedictine Abbey all around and spectacular views up towards St. Catherine's Chapel high up on a grassy hill to the west. A barn to the south is the main survivor from the Abbey days and is undoubtedly one of the largest such buildings in the country. It dates from the beginning of the fifteenth century and would have appealed to **William Morris** with his love for similar buildings such as his beloved Great Coxwell barn in Oxfordshire.

The church's oldest parts date from a similar period with much modification to the interior occurring during the nineteenth century when the west gallery and the (now removed) north gallery were built.

In the south chapel there is stained glass by **Robert Anning Bell** which was installed in 1910 in memory of the Fifth Earl of Ilchester. It has the figure of St *Catherine* in the centre with the figures of St *Nicholas* and St *Andrew* to either side.

The interior of the church also has a marvellous classical reredos dating from the middle of the eighteenth century and a Jacobean pulpit with sounding board. There is a patterned Victorian encaustic tiled pavement in the chancel area.

The church is open most days.

ABBOTSBURY BARN

ATHELHAMPTON is just over six miles north-east of Dorchester off the A35.

ATHELHAMPTON HOUSE is a fine late medieval manor house which has wallpaper on the stairs and landing that has some similarities to the **William Morris** tapestry design called *Pineapple*. Elsewhere in the house are a number of Puginesque wallpapers some appearing to be older than others. Also there are a number of other artefacts inspired by **Augustus Welby Northmore Pugin** including a font and candelabra. In addition there are sculptured busts of Queen Victoria and Prince Albert with a statue of Victoria to be seen in the impressive gardens. These were largely planned by Inigo Thomas in the 1890s. It is not known if **Pugin** himself was involved in the installation of the interior furnishings.

The house is open between March 1st. to October 31st. from Sunday to Thursday 11-5.

Near a tollhouse can be seen the CHURCH OF ST. JOHN which was built by John Hicks of Dorchester in 1861-2 and whom was a friend and architectural colleague of Thomas Hardy.

The church may occasionally be locked but access is possible through the church wardens.

ATHELHAMPTON HOUSE

BEAMINSTER lies about eight miles north of Bridport along the A3066.

The CHURCH OF ST MARY appears to have been much altered internally in recent years with for example the pulpit being placed unceremoniously at the west end of the south aisle. However it does have some nice Victorian painted corbels (apparently by the firm of Burge and Allen who also designed corbels for the House of Commons) in the nave and two stained glass windows from the **Kempe** stable. These are both to be found in the south aisle. The oldest depicts the *Saints Michael, George* and *Alban* and dates from 1885. The window adjacent dates from 1931 and so well after the death of

Charles Eamer Kempe and consequently the work of **C.E.Kempe & Co. Ltd.** *It shows the Virgin Mary with King David and St Luke.*
  The church is open most days.

KEMPE & CO. GLASS IN BEAMINSTER CHURCH

HORN PARK is about one and a half miles north of Beaminster along the A3066.
  An Art and Crafts house with a neo-Georgian bent designed by **T. Lawrence Dale** in 1911. The house sits prettily within its sixty-six acres.
  Private house.

BERE REGIS is approximately halfway between Poole and Dorchester on the A35.

The CHURCH OF ST. JOHN THE BAPTIST contains extensive floor tiling by **William Godwin** dating from 1875 when **George Edmund Street** completed his restoration of the building. The encaustic pavement is based on medieval armorial designs known to have been used in the church as well as a design used on a large medieval tile found at nearby Bindon Abbey. In the church only one original tile remains.

  Also dating from the Victorian period and worthy of interest are the set of stained glass windows by **John Hardman & Co.** particularly those showing an ethereal quality with figures in their silvery robes with golden haloes.

  The embroidery on the altar frontal shows the influence of **William Morris.**

  Look up to see one of the finest timber church roofs in Dorset with its carved figures (possibly representing the *Twelve Apostles*) and ornamental bosses. Dating from the fifteenth century the roof appears to have hammerbeams but in fact it is of tiebeam construction with much decoration on the arched braces. The exuberant colours of the roof may not be as old and most likely date only from **Street's** time when the stone chancel screen and wooden pews also arrived.
  The church is open most days.

TILES AND ALTAR FRONTAL AT BERE REGIS

BOTHENHAMPTON is just under a mile south of Bridport on the B3157.

The old Church of the Holy Trinity was partially demolished in 1886 as it was in a state of decay and was not in any case of adequate size to serve an expanding population. This action only took place after The Society for the Protection of Ancient Buildings (SPAB) had been consulted and approved a proposal to construct a new church. SPAB had been founded by **William Morris** and others about ten years before because of their concerns about the vulnerability of old buildings to destruction and modification and to the practice of 'restoration' so popular at the time. Nevertheless the Society clearly agreed with the arguments placed before them to replace this church at Bothenhampton. So **Morris** himself was probably personally involved in the decision to retain parts of the old church and to construct a new building on a different site.

The new HOLY TRINITY CHURCH was built between 1887-9 by **Edward Schroeder Prior** who was then in his mid-thirties and was fresh from completing his distinctive Pier Terrace at West Bay just down the road. He had family in the Bridport area, so it is perhaps not a total surprise that he was appointed to the task but it does mean that Dorset has a very early example of an Arts and Crafts church. The outside of the building is essentially Gothic in style and unassuming, although it does occupy a pleasant elevated site. It is only when one enters the church that its loftiness becomes apparent a fact emphasized by **Prior's** use of arches-not just the three giant ones in the nave-but also the highly pitched chancel Gothic arch and the deep recessed arches of the windows and organ opening. The use of the arches here provided **Prior** with practical experience which he would later combine with his developing architectural skills to produce what many people consider to be his masterpiece in a larger scale at his church at Roker in County Durham. That church is noted for its chancel roof decoration by Macdonald Gill (Eric's brother) and interestingly the stone pulpit here seems to have been decorated by the same man but was enclosed by oak panelling in 1904. Other furnishings include the altar which was designed by **Prior** and has a gesso front by **William Lethaby**. The three lights and trefoil of the east window are by **Christopher Whall** and as at Burton Bradstock his work appears here probably at the request of **Prior**. They date from about 1896 and are therefore early examples of **Whall's** design style. At the west end there are two lancets and a roundel by the firm of Jones and Willis. The wrought iron screen between the chancel and nave with the words *Sanctus Sanctus Sanctus* is by a local man F. W. Grange.

The church is open most days.

BOTHENHAMPTON CHURCH INTERIOR

BOURNEMOUTH is situated on the coastline midway between Poole and Christchurch being a little less than six miles from either. It was in the county of Hampshire until 1974 when a reorganisation of local government brought it into Dorset.

William Morris visited the town in 1882 where his daughter Jenny was staying. He seems to have designed a wallpaper pattern whilst there and wrote to his daughter to tell her he was thinking about calling it *Christ –Church* in preference to Bournemouth. This was probably a private joke of some sort between Jenny and her father.

A year later **Morris** followed up a previous remark on the poverty of good houses to be found in the town in a letter to Catherine Holiday the wife of **Henry Holiday** saying *'I don't know that the builders at Bournemouth are worse than at other places except that there has been a desperate hurry there to run up houses for Podsnap, Bounderby, Gradgrind and company-heaps of money to be made'.* A comment no doubt about the rapid development of Bournemouth by Dickensian type speculators.

The architectural historian Nikolaus Pevsner also thought the domestic architecture of the town was *'consistently undistinguished'* and had a mixed opinion about its churches but it is largely within these buildings that work by the Pre-Raphaelite and Arts and Crafts movements can be found.

The CHURCH OF ST. AUGUSTINE (in Wimborne Road) was built in 1891-2 by **William Butterfield**. At the west end is stained glass designed by **Karl Parsons** and fitted by **Lowndes & Drury** in 1931.

The church may be locked but access is possible through the church wardens.

The CHURCH OF ST. CLEMENT is found in St Clement's Road Boscombe and was largely built in 1871-3 with **John Dando Sedding** as the architect. Much influenced by the Arts and Crafts movement it was his first major work and was the result of family contacts. He married the sister of the first vicar of the church.

The most interesting feature of the exterior of St. Clements is the west front of the tower although this was only finally finished two years after the architect's death in 1891. **Henry Wilson** was mainly responsible for this as he was in a number of projects left unfinished by the time of **Sedding's** early death. The window here has wonderful tracery in an art nouveau style and there is a statue by Frederick William Pomeroy.

In the south-eastern corner of the churchyard are three gravestones designed by **Sedding** under the names of Tinling (the first vicar) and Scurfield and dating from the early eighteen eighties.

The interior of the church is bright and filled with furnishings of great quality. **Sedding's** decorative scheme is very striking and very evident in the encaustic tiling that extends from the nave to the chancel and Lady Chapel. The lectern is also designed by

him (1876) as is the stained glass in the Lady Chapel which was made by N.H.J. Westlake who was also responsible for the west window (1883). The nave is a veritable who's who of Victorian glass with examples of the work of **Christopher Whall** (who worked a good deal in collaboration with **Sedding**), H.W. Bryans and an *Annunciation* and *Presentation* by **C.E. Kempe & Co. Ltd.** on the south side (1919). The previously mentioned west window in the tower has a very satisfying design by **Henry Holiday.**

If the church is locked access can be made through the church wardens.

The CHURCH OF ST PETER (Hinton Road) has without doubt one of the finest Victorian interiors in the county. The wonderful decorative complexity apparent when one enters the building, leads to an initial sense of being overwhelmed by it all but it is soon possible to appreciate the many individual features of the highest artistic merit.

In 1853 **George Edmund Street** was asked to build a new church here

DETAIL OF ST. CLEMENT'S CHURCH TOWER

but he chose to keep aspects of an original building already on the site around which he designed a much larger church. He was a young man at the time and St. Peter's was his first commission for a town church.

The first stage of this project was the construction of a north aisle which was completed around 1856. Here are twelve lancet windows showing the *Apostles* positioned very close together and thus catching the eye, although they are at odds with those in the original south aisle opposite where the stained glass is more spaced out. The glass in the north aisle was designed by A.Gibbs in 1856 whilst that on the south side is by William Wailes and dating mainly from four years earlier.

Between 1855-9 **Street** completed the nave and clerestory after which he could dismantle the roof of the original building. The nave has magnificent fresco work by **Clayton & Bell** over the chancel arch showing the *Crucifixion* and dating from 1873. Further frescos were added four years later to the area over the nave arches. The octagonal font is one of a number of quite exquisite sculptural works by **Thomas Earp** that can be found in the church.

The chancel and transepts were the next part of the building to be finished (1864) and not surprisingly it is in these areas and in the sanctuary that the decorative scheme reaches new heights of richness. Here there are roof decorations and stone vaulting to **Bodley's** designs and also frescos by him in the sanctuary (1886-91). The high altar has a reredos by **Earp** which is of the highest order and this is flanked on both sides by mosaic tiles depicting Pre-Raphaelite angels with musical instruments. These date from 1899 and were designed by Arthur Blomfield and produced by **James Powell & Sons.**

Lovely as they are these tiles replaced some others which were of more historical note but these had virtually disintegrated in the short time they spent in situ. The tile set that was previously either side of the altar was a far rarer commodity having come from the workshops of **Morris & Co.** and commissioned by **Street**, whose pupil **Morris**, had spent time in his architect offices. The tiles were similar in subject matter with three angels in procession and the designs had been used before in stained glass but usually not together. **Street** in fact ordered stained glass (see below) as well as six different sets of tiles for St. Peter's. The other four sets of tiles were for the north and south walls of the chancel with scenes entitled *Feeding the Five Thousand, Supper at Emmaus* (south side) and *The Last Supper* and *The Marriage at Cana* (north wall). These panels were about one yard square a little smaller than the ones near the high altar. There are watercolour sketches and drawings for these tiles, so some idea can be obtained as to how they looked in the church but alas there is no direct evidence of how the tiles looked in their completed form. Only the altar tiles appear in an archive church photograph. It seems all the tiles quickly deteriorated leading to their removal and in the case of the altar tiles their replacement. The only other **Morris** tiles to be found in an ecclesiastical setting are in two churches in Sussex.

Before moving on to the south transept, look at the impressive east window designed by **Street** and produced by **Clayton & Bell** in 1866. There are also further sculptural reliefs by **Earp** to be seen high up in the choir arcade.

Passing through one of **Street's** wrought iron and brass screens, the Keble Chapel can be found named after John Keble one of the members of the Oxford Movement who worshipped in this church until his death in the town in 1866. The Oxford Movement were a group of high church Anglicans who emphasised the importance of ceremony in their worship, bringing them closer to Roman Catholic principles. Keble can be seen complete with cassock and hood in the lower right-hand corner of the *Te Deum* window in the south transept (**Clayton & Bell,** 1867).

South of the altar in the chapel and therefore a little hidden away is the early **Morris** glass commissioned by **Street** and installed in 1864. The three lights depict scenes from Jesus on the sea of Tiberius. From left to right the panels show *Christ Walking on the Water, The Miraculous Draught of Fishes* and *The Miracle of the Loaves and Fishes.* All the designs are by **Burne-Jones** with the quarries and border by **Philip Webb.** None of the designs had been used previously. The reredos and wall paintings in the chapel were added in 1907-8 when the area was refurbished and are the work of **Heaton, Butler & Bayne.**

Elsewhere in the church more glass of interest by **Clayton & Bell** and **Ninian Comper** can be found in the Annunciation Chapel together with fine carving by **Earp.** But in regards to this sculptor it is his pulpit designed by **Street** that provides his tour de force.

There is yet further fine work by **Comper, Clayton & Bell** and T. G. Jackson throughout the interior and outside there are the graves of the poet Percy Bysshe Shelley and his wife Mary Shelley.

Street completed the building of the church in 1879 with the completion of the spire adjacent to which are four more figures carved by **Earp.** All in all, the church provides the visitor with many impressive examples of Victorian skill and endeavour and direct evidence of the increasing influence of Pre-Raphaelite art in the period from the eighteen-fifties to the early twentieth century.

The church is open most days.

Unusually both John Betjeman and Nikolaus Pevsner agreed that the CHURCH OF ST STEPHEN (St. Stephen's Way) is the most significant church in Bournemouth the former describing it as the *'most beautiful'* and Pevsner saying it was *'the finest'*.

CHANCEL OF ST.PETER'S

Building started in 1881 and most of the church was completed by 1898 with the exception of the tower. The architect was **John Loughborough Pearson** with his son Frank finishing the tower by 1907. Frank was also responsible for some of the fine furnishings including the ironwork surrounding the font and the choir stalls. His father had died in 1897 leaving Frank to complete a number of his buildings including arguably his most prestigious work, Truro Cathedral.

By the time **Pearson** came to St Stephen's, he had honed his talents to virtual perfection, enhancing the space at Bournemouth by placing the columns in the chancel a little further in giving an illusion that the building is longer and higher than in reality. In his lifetime, **Pearson** came into conflict with **William Morris** and SPAB on occasion such as in 1883 when he was

MORRIS & CO. WINDOW IN ST PETER'S

consulted in regard to the west front of Peterborough Cathedral. At the time, this was in an appalling state and **Morris, Lethaby, Webb, Prior, Ashbee** and many other sympathisers advocated repairing the front using largely invisible means, whereas **Pearson** and his supporters wished to use some new stones where old ones could no longer be used and thus recreate the façade as it was in Norman times. **Pearson** won the argument and today we would most likely feel his approach was not too far removed from current ideas of restoration.

At Bournemouth there are also examples of the work of **Nathaniel Hitch** as seen in the pulpit and in particular the reredos above his carved altar. It may have been through another sculptor Thomas Nicholls that **Hitch** first met **J.L. Pearson**. This meeting was the start of an enduring partnership and the sculptor completed nearly thirty commissions for **Pearson** in the period 1885-1896 including his work at St Stephen's.

Another sculptor's work can be admired in the Lady Chapel in the form of an alabaster Virgin and Child. This is by **Benjamin Clemens.**

The church is open most days.

HUME TOWERS of Branksome Wood Road is now long demolished but was built for Sir Joshua Walmsley a politician and corn broker in 1870-1. Following his death soon afterwards and that of his widow in 1873 the house passed to W.E.Cooper who wrote extensively on health matters and notably on the benefits of vegetarianism at around the turn of the twentieth century. In 1901 **Morris & Co.** supplied a series of windows to this gentleman with subjects based on the planets including *Morning Star, Evening Star, Sol, Luna, Mars, Venus* and *Jupiter.* Also in the same year **Morris & Co.** supplied a number of windows with the figures of poets as subjects and first used in the Combination Room at Peterhouse College in Cambridge in 1872-4. The designs (originally by **Burne-Jones**) were *Homer, Aeschylus, Virgil, Horace, Dante* and *Chaucer.* Lastly, a set of five minstrel

PULPIT IN ST STEPHEN'S CHURCH

figures was supplied again in 1901 and based on the *Minstrel Angel* figures often used in the tracery of church windows but supplied without wings for domestic use.

Later it seems the building was used as a hospital for returning soldiers in World War I who were experiencing psychiatric problems. Only some of the **Morris** windows appear to have survived the changes in use of Hume Towers, the bombing of the town in World War II and its subsequent demolition, these being the *Homer, Aeschylus* and *Virgil* figures and the minstrel figures albeit in a damaged state.

There is a further entry in the **Morris & Co.** catalogue of designs which refers to twenty-seven panels of painted quarries being supplied to 'Gablehurst'. These have not been traced but there was a house of the same name in Branksome Park built in about 1884 by the architect J. Nixon Horsfield.

Also rather intriguingly, a set of ten planet windows of which no complete set is known were supplied to 'Woodlands' in 1878 and although these are all untraced there does appear to have been a villa of the same name in Branksome Wood Road.

These houses have been demolished.

THE RUSSELL-COTES ART GALLERY AND MUSEUM (East Cliff Promenade/Russell Cotes Road) has a large collection of Victorian art and sculpture set within a palatial building of the time with lovely sea views. Please see separate chapter for full details.

The museum is open 10-5 Tuesday to Sunday and Bank Holiday Mondays.

BRIANTSPUDDLE is about eleven miles east of Dorchester off the A35.

This charming village has many white walled and thatched cottages of varying age. One of the most distinctive collections of buildings is found at the eastern end of the village. Originally built as a dairy farm THE RING is a group of linked one and two storeyed cottages around an oval green. They were built in 1919 by Ernest Debenham (the department store entrepreneur) with some flair and this can be seen particularly in the brick trimmed turrets and their caps of thatch. The cottages were built using local materials and there are other examples of Debenham's work to be found throughout the village. He himself had a country estate centred on Moreton House close to the village and he hoped to set up a model farm there to stop agricultural workers leaving the area to work in the towns and cities.

If you follow the road that heads westwards out of Briantspuddle you soon arrive at the hamlet of Bladen Valley largely located down a cul-de-sac on the left-hand side. The originator of these houses is again Ernest Debenham with designs by Halsey Ricardo and MacDonald (Max) Gill.

THE RING AT BRIANTSPUDDLE

It is however the striking WAR MEMORIAL by MacDonald's illustrious brother **Eric Gill** that is hard to ignore. The figure of *Christ* is shown with a large sword and this depiction of Christ was **Gill's** first attempt at the figure. During, and after the end of the First World War, the Imperial War Graves Commission asked **Gill** to complete a number of war memorials to be sited in British villages and the Briantspuddle one is an example of these. It was commissioned by Debenham in 1915 and in addition to the fore-mentioned figure of *Christ* there is a statue of the *Madonna and Child* under a canopy on the south side of the monument. The memorial is constructed of Portland and Purbeck stone and **Gill** worked on it in situ. The unusual inscription around the base is by the fifteenth century mystic Julian of Norwich.

BRIDPORT is just over six miles south of Beaminster.

In the CHURCH OF ST MARY (South Street) is a memorial in the form of an oval marble tablet to Harriet Templer completed by **Eric Gill** in 1906. The inscription uses his characteristic 'R' with its curve to the leg and the alabaster frame has examples of his leaf design.

Nearby in Bradpole (to the north-east of the town) there is more of **Gill's** work in the churchyard of the HOLY TRINITY church. This is a ledgerstone in memory of William Hounsell that dates from about 1903. It has been suggested that the layout of the inscription is one of the most eccentric of **Gill's** with the lettering divided up by the arms of the cross.

The churches may be locked but access is possible through the church wardens.

BRYANSTON lies a little to the west of Blandford Forum which is eighteen miles north-west of Poole along the A350.

It is possible to drive through the estate where this **Norman Shaw** house of the 1890s was built. It is Shaw working in a neo-Wren style and unfortunately the whole view of the house has been marred by more recent ugly development.

The house now forms part of a boarding school.

DETAIL OF THE GILL MEMORIAL AT BRIANTSPUDDLE

BUCKLAND NEWTON is about twelve miles north of Dorchester along the B3143.

The CHURCH OF THE HOLY ROOD has a three-lighted west window by window depicting the Saints *Michael, Gabriel and Raphael*. The glass is by **C.E. Kempe & Co. Ltd.** and dates from 1916. Disappointingly it is now obscured by the new organ but an illustration of it can be seen in the church guide.

The church is normally open during daylight hours.

BURTON BRADSTOCK is just less than four miles to the south-east of Bridport along the B3157.

Like many churches the CHURCH OF ST MARY is a product of a few centuries, however internally much of what you see today dates from a major restoration in 1897. This was overseen by **E. S. Prior** who was by this time well established as an architect working within the Arts and Crafts movement. But it was a local connection that provided one of the main reasons for his work at Burton Bradstock. He was the cousin of the rector James Lethbridge Templer and twelve years earlier had married Isabella Maunsell the daughter of the Vicar of Symondsbury. He had also previously been involved in a couple of projects in the county as a result of these familial arrangements- specifically three buildings at West Bay and the church at Bothenhampton (see separate entries in this book). His work here was more modest and was primarily concerned with rebuilding the south aisle and providing a new south door with associated woodwork. The modifications are highly accomplished to the extent that they blend in seamlessly with

DETAIL OF THE WHALL WINDOW AT BURTON BRADSTOCK

SOME OF THE WALL DECORATION AT BURTON BRADSTOCK

the earlier fabric of the building. This means that the most obvious aspect of **Prior's** work to be seen today, is the distinctive glass in his replacement windows. These can be admired in both the north and south aisles where his thick but largely clear glass lets in ample quantities of light. The minimalistic floral design of the south windows is particularly pleasing.

Opposite is a bold window by another designer associated with the Art and Crafts movement **Christopher Whall** whose use of dark but iridescent colour against clear quarries of glass produces elements of the dramatic. The window dates from 1923 and has *Christ in Majesty* in its central light.

The seating in the nave is a little unusual being oak benches made by a Mr Haywood who lived locally. The wall panelling just above was made from the previous box pews and decorated and inscribed by the wife of the rector with help from members of the parish.

The church is open most days.

CATHERSTON LEWESTON is five and a half miles to the north-east of Lyme Regis on the A3052 and then via Charmouth.

Follow the approach to the manor house and the small CHURCH OF ST MARY soon appears on the right-hand side. Designed by **J. L. Pearson** in 1858 the building is nothing exceptional although everything is completed to a high standard. This is most

noticeable in the flint work and in the exquisite stone carving to be seen by the entrance. But it can also be seen in the attention to detail throughout the interior from the woodwork of the ceiling to the tiling pavement and attractive reredos. The glass is by **Clayton & Bell** and fits perfectly into a space that is pure Victorian Gothic Revival.

The church is open most days.

CATTISTOCK is about nine miles east of Beaminster via the B3163 and A356.

The CHURCH OF ST PETER AND ST PAUL is a place of pilgrimage for many and in particular for lovers of the Pre-Raphaelites and the Arts and Crafts movement and provides a fine reason (even on its own) for visiting Dorset. The building is mainly Victorian but in the most thrilling manner. The men responsible for such an arresting edifice were **Sir George Gilbert Scott** and his eldest son **George Jnr.** The work was started in 1857 by **Scott Snr.** whereby he added a south aisle to an original building

CATHERSTON LEWESTON DOORWAY

and also a polygonal apse. In addition he modified the nave and took down a gallery but these changes were modest in comparison to his son's work starting from 1874. He constructed a new tower based on the one at Charminster and interestingly placed his baptistery in its base. This area is the most delightful partly for being so unexpected. It is lined with murals designed by Temple Moore (a pupil of **Scott Jnr.**) in 1901-6 who also made the grandiose font cover. On one wall of the lofty space is *St George* on horseback (the church guide suggests this could be by W.O. and C. Powell) whilst opposite a more **Morrisian** type of decoration can be viewed. There are foliage patterns and heraldic shields set within architectural features such as a window and arch. One wall is satisfyingly divided into panels with two sets of four figures alternating with foliage and text in a manner very reminiscent of a stained glass window.

Elsewhere in the interior are a number of other charming features. Foremost amongst these is the **Morris & Co.** window of 1882 at the western end of the south aisle. This is in its own small way a touch of perfection. The two lights each have three angelic figures one above the other with backgrounds of deep and pale blue with white stars. The figures are united by all having red wings and scrolls beneath them. At the top of the left light is *St Michael*, the other descending figures on that side being entitled *Praying Angel* and *Minstrel Angel*. The first figure is to a **Burne-Jones** design and the other two are from the hand of **Morris** himself. On the right-hand side beginning at the top is *Guardian Angel*, then *Censing Angel* and below another variation of a *Minstrel Angel*. Once again only the top figure was designed by **Burne-Jones** with the other two angels being by **Morris**. With its borders of alternate crowns and leaves and bold use of colour the window really impresses particularly on a sunny day. It's worth noting that none of the

CATTISTOCK CHURCH

DECORATION AT CATTISTOCK

figures were designed specially for this location-the top two being adapted from the *Angels of the Hierarchy* window at Jesus College Chapel in Cambridge and the middle pair were first used on the ceiling of the same chapel. The two lowest figures are adaptations of the ones to be seen in the south chancel window at St John's church in Tuebrook, Liverpool.

Another window in the south aisle is by **C.E. Kempe & Co.** and although not in the same league as the **Morris** is a decent enough *Annunciation* dating from 1917 and in memory of Frank Ewart Savill of nearby Chantmarle Manor.

The main west window could be by **Clayton & Bell** but it is also possible that it emanates from the workshops of the Burlison & Grylls stained glass company.

In the north transept is a later east window (1923) by **Robert Anning Bell** depicting *St Dorothy.*

The chancel has tiles by **Minton** with those near the altar being a serene blue and white. It is also worth noting the wrought iron gates here and the alabaster figure of Christ in the middle of a wooden reredos. This is the sole remainder of **Scott's** original tiled reredos.

Before departing it is well worth exploring the information folders kept in the north transept that contain correspondence between experts such as Gavin Stamp and Martin Harrison about the origins of some of the artefacts in this lovely church.

The church is open most days.

DETAIL OF THE KEMPE & CO. WINDOW AT CHARMINSTER

CHARMINSTER is a little over two miles to the north of Dorchester via short stretches of the B3147, A37 and A352.

The CHURCH OF ST. MARY has a particularly bold tower which was built by Sir Thomas Trenchard of nearby Wolfeton in the sixteenth century. The more modest chancel was constructed in 1838 and replaced a medieval one which was demolished in the seventeenth century due to decay. In the same year the north aisle was enlarged and further much needed remedial work was done by C.E. Ponting in 1895-7.

The west window dates from this time (1896) and is by **C.E. Kempe**, it depicts the *Madonna and Child* with *Angels* to either side and below is *St Michael* with scenes from *The Annunciation* and *The Angel appearing before the Shepherds* across five lights. It is a window of the highest order with stunning details. Also in the church is glass by Burlison & Grylls (1912) in the east window.

The church is open most days.

CHARMOUTH is on the coast a little east of Lyme Regis.

THISTLEGATE HOUSE is an Arts and Crafts domestic building of red brick in a style similar to work by **Lutyens**. The architect was **F.W.Troup** in 1911.

The house is private.

CHILD OKEFORD is about seven and a half miles to the north-west of Blandford Forum along the A350 and A357.

The CHURCH OF ST NICHOLAS dates from Victorian times with the exception of its tower which is late fifteenth or early sixteenth century. Once inside the building it is the chancel walls that beg for attention lined as they are with marble installed in 1912.

The chancel also contains three stained glass windows by Henry Hughes (1822-83) of the company Ward & Hughes. From the 1860s Hughes produced windows under his own name as well as for the firm where he was chief designer. There is further glass by Hughes in the east window of the Lady Chapel.

In a more Pre-Raphaelite vein are the two windows by the Jersey designer **Henry Thomas Bosdet** to be found opposite one another in the south and north aisles. The former has two lights showing the *Archangel Gabriel* and *Mary* whilst the north window depicts *St George, King David* and *St Maurice*. Both windows date from 1920 when **Bosdet** had a glass making studio in Chiswick. There are quite a few of his windows to be found in churches on his home island.

Also to be found in the south window of the Lady Chapel is a work by **C. E. Kempe** that dates from 1888 and is therefore quite early. It is called the Magnificat Window and shows

DETAIL OF THE BOSDET GLASS AT CHILD OKEFORD

Hannah and her child *Samuel* on the left with the *Virgin Mary* and the infant *Christ* on the right-hand side.

The church is open most days.

CHRISTCHURCH is found on the coast to the eastern side of Bournemouth. The town was part of Hampshire until 1974 when it came into Dorset.

The CHURCH OF ST. GEORGE was dedicated in 1928 and replaced a tin church that was previously located in Brighton. It was transported down to Christchurch in sections by rail and wagon. Once inside the present church the **Morris** glass is to be found in the chancel in the form of two single lights. These show *St Paul* on the left with the patron saint of the church *St George* to the right. The windows date from 1930 and are both to the designs of **Burne-Jones** being used here in most likelihood for the last time in stained glass. Both designs first appeared in the medium some fifty years earlier. The church can be found in Jumpers Road just off Barrack Road (A35).

The church may be locked but access is possible through the church wardens.

The PRIORY CHURCH houses a number of artefacts closely or indirectly associated with the Pre-Raphaelites. The most obvious is an early painting by **Millais** to be found by turning left just after entering the building through its main entrance. Here beneath the tower are in fact two sections of a painting which originally made up the greater part of a larger composition. They now have the titles, *The Rich Young Ruler* and *The Widow's Mite* but appeared initially under the latter title, when they formed the majority of a large picture entered for the 1847 Westminster Hall competition for the decoration of the Houses of Parliament. The original composition depicted *Christ* standing against a blaze of light and calling to *St. John's* notice a woman's act of unselfishness.

In 1846 **Millais** had been working on the painting when **Hunt** visited his studio. He had come there at the former's invitation following a discussion the pair had in a hall at the Royal Academy. **Millais** had said, *'Look here, you know I'm painting a picture as big as Raphael's Cartoons, 9 feet one way by 16 feet the other. That's no end of a job I can tell you. Twenty figures and more, all the size of life'.* He continued, *'It's 'The Widow's Mite'- it's a splendid subject, isn't it? You know there are the old frowning Pharisees, the reverential disciples, and the poor woman, giving all she's got, and of course there's the Saviour'* (quoted from Pre-Raphaelitism and The Pre-Raphaelite Brotherhood by **William Holman Hunt**). During Hunt's visit he met the younger artist's mother and father, the latter of which had modelled for several of the doctors in the painting. There was also discussion about how **Millais's** brother William had sat for the figure of *St. John* and how a servant working in Bedford Square was found for the head of *Christ*.

Unfortunately, the picture was not a great success as the critics of the day objected to the widow holding a nude child thinking this to be in poor taste. It was subsequently cut up, the two main panels being thought to have been separated but these are most likely those now on view in the Priory and donated by Mrs. Eleanor Reeves in 1928. They were shown in the groundbreaking retrospective exhibition organised by the Walker Art Gallery in Liverpool in 1967 an event that signalled a revival of interest in the work of the Pre-Raphaelites.

Adjacent to the two paintings by **Millais** is the memorial to the poet Percy Bysshe Shelley designed by **Henry Weekes** in 1853-4 and originally intended for the churchyard at St. Peter's in Bournemouth. It shows the man who provided such inspiration to a later generation of Pre-Raphaelite poets in the arms of his second wife the author Mary Wollstonecraft Shelley. The monument was commissioned by Shelley's son Sir Percy Shelley and his wife after the death of Mary Shelley. Although **Weekes** in his lifetime distanced himself from sculpture that was excessively naturalistic his depiction of the drowned poet shows him very naturalistically still wet having presumably been just brought out of the sea.

Also to be found within the walls of the Priory are two connections to the life of **Augustus Welby Northmore Pugin.** When only thirteen he was dispatched to Christchurch following an illness. The town may have been chosen as it was the native town of Benjamin Ferrey later a busy architect but then a fellow pupil in the studio of **Pugin's** father. The town appealed to the young man and he even wondered about building a house by the sea and took the opportunity to collect interesting objects in the local antiquity shops. He also completed a sketch that reveals a nautical interest showing as it does a number of sea boats in front of the Priory.

In 1831 when he was nineteen he married his first wife Anne Garnet who tragically died only a year later following the birth of a daughter, Anne. A grieving husband chose to bury his wife here and there is a memorial brass on a black marble slab designed by **Pugin** near the Berkeley Chantry. Also dating from the same year is a communion table in the north transept made by him and presented to the Priory but simplified from its original rather extravagant drawing. It is still an item of furniture full of rich carving although his friend Ferrey thought it may have lacked the right expression for an ecclesiastical piece. Ferrey restored the Priory in 1862.

Elsewhere in this vast building there are windows by Lavers & Barraud at the west end and in the east window of the Draper Chapel. The windows date from the early eighteen-sixties.

The priory is open most days.

CHRISTCHURCH PRIORY

The WORKSHOP AND BOW FRONTED SHOP where **Arthur Romney Green** established himself from 1920 until his death can still be seen in Christchurch where it is now an Italian restaurant. There is a blue plaque on the building and examples of Green's furniture can be seen in the local Red House museum.

The premises are in Bridge Street.

Readers with some time on their hands might like to consider a trip to Thorney Hill a few miles to the north-east across the border in Hampshire. ALL SAINTS CHURCH was designed by **Detmar Blow** who in his earlier days was an architect working in the Art and Crafts style. Although this church dates from 1906 and has Baroque tendencies it does contain the last mural to be designed by **Phoebe Traquair** completed in 1922. The subject is the *Te Deum* and the magnificent composition includes figures such as Tennyson, Blake and Pasteur set within a New Forest landscape. **Traquair** had a key role in the development of the Arts and Crafts movement particularly in Edinburgh and during her lifetime exhibited her work widely. Also in the interior of the church is sculpture by **Eric Gill** and Bertram MacKennal.

The church may be locked but access is possible through the church wardens.

The building and much of its contents were commissioned by the Manners family of Avon Tyrell a large Art and Crafts house nearby that was designed and furnished by **W.R. Lethaby** from 1891. The house was constructed on land owned by Lord Manner's wife Constance Fane and the couple's eldest son John Neville was painted by **Millais** late in his career. The painting was exhibited at the Royal Academy in 1896. **Ernest Gimson** carried out plaster decoration in many of the main rooms in the house.

The house is private.

COLEHILL is a couple of miles or so to the north-east of Wimborne Minster.

The CHURCH OF ST. MICHAEL AND ALL ANGELS was designed by **W.D. Caroe** during 1891 with work starting two years later and the building being consecrated in 1895. It is undoubtedly one of the more unusual churches in the county with various commentators from architectural historians to local writers suggesting over the years that it would be more at home elsewhere in places such as Surrey, California and Scandinavia. This is despite it being described as *'old English style and suitable to the surroundings'* in the original plans.

The building is of red brick with half timbering in black and white appearing in the gables and dormers as well as in features such as the porch and tower. Inside there is a large timber roof which is stained dark green and which in the south aisle and chancel chapel becomes frankly eccentric in design.

There are some wonderful individual features to be explored within the building. One of the most striking is the pear wood or oak figure of *St. Michael* set within a brick niche. The statue is said to be by an Italian sculptor G. Pucci. Perhaps he also had a role to play in how the font in the baptistery came to be here-it is made of marble which could have come from Italy and is another example of the eclectic nature of the church's contents. Almost next door to the statue is the lectern with its baroque cherubs which again initially seems stylistically to be out of place, but later just seems to blend in with the other artefacts in a fascinating interior. In the sanctuary are four embroidered angels that together form the altar frontal-they were completed by four ladies in the parish in the early twentieth century but which could easily have been designed by **William Morris** himself. Back in the chancel the elaborate organ case contains some fine carving.

At the time of writing the east window was removed for restoration purposes and replaced with boarding hence the sanctuary area was quite gloomy. The glass that can usually be seen is by **Ninian Comper** and depicts the four Archangels plus *St. George* and *St. Nicholas*. It should look pristine when it is returned to the building. There is also a reredos to be found just in front of the window showing the *Nativity* but because of the ongoing repairs taking place at the time of visiting this could not be viewed.

The exterior of the church is restless and busy but never fails to satisfy. In particular the view of the tower and gables from the north-east shows very well what an original design **Caroe** brought to fruition at Colehill. Even the north wall which was only expected to be temporary (in the event of a north aisle being built to match the one in the south) is a work of skill alternating glass with black and white decoration.

The church may be locked but access can usually be made through contact with the church wardens.

EMBROIDERED ANGELS IN COLEHILL CHURCH

CRANBORNE is about ten miles to the north-west of Ringwood via the B3081 and the B3078.

Cranborne is mentioned in Thomas Hardy's *Tess of the d'Urbervilles* under the name of Chaseborough where the novel's heroine rested on her way to Trantridge (Pentridge).

The CHURCH OF ST. PETER AND ST. BARTHOLOMEW has an initial impact on a visitor by way of its sheer scale and in particular its massive tower. Its size is explained by the building's earlier history as part of a Priory broken up at the time of the Dissolution of the Monasteries during the reign of Henry VIII.

Of particular interest in the interior of the present building are the examples of woodcarving by the Rev. F.H. Fisher who was the vicar here from 1888 until 1910. His work includes the chancel and tower screens as well as the reredos in the Lady Chapel the latter being perhaps his most exquisite piece. The leaves of the plants on the four central sections of the latter are impressively naturalistic and would no doubt have found approval with **John Ruskin** had he viewed them and his doctrine to seek Truth in Nature. On the south side of the church is a window in the vicar's memory-although this and other stained glass are not especially memorable and not inspired by ideas associated with the Arts and Crafts movement. However the window of four lights also on the south wall in memory of John Tregonwell is of interest as many people feel he was responsible for founding Bournemouth, a town notable for its Victorian churches. After perhaps looking at the very old oak pulpit with its monogram 'TP' probably standing for Thomas Parker, an Abbot hereabouts in 1381-1421 step back outside.

More work appropriate to the Arts and Crafts is to be found west of the tower in the form of a gravestone designed by **Eric Gill**. This is to the memory of Michael C.J. Cecil and is found with other headstones of the same family. The stone dates from 1937.

The church is open most days.

WOODCARVING AT CRANBORNE

DORCHESTER is equidistant between Poole and Lyme Regis along the A35.
The south chapel in DORCHESTER CEMETERY is found in Weymouth Avenue.
The east window of three lights shows *The Crucifixion* and can be viewed with some difficulty through a window in the north wall as the chapel is often locked. The two lights either side of the main scene show events that occurred after *The Crucifixion*. There are in addition tracery lights depicting angels. The glass was made in memory of a local solicitor and was installed in 1890. A little surprisingly, in view of its preponderance of bright colours, it is the work of **Christopher Whall** who would have had his own studio in Dorking, Surrey by this time, following on from the period he worked for **James Powell & Sons.**
The chapel is often locked when not in use.
The CHURCH OF ST GEORGE is located in Fordington which is now a locale found within the town. It greatly increased in size in the earlier years of the twentieth century and its evolving nature is reflected in the presentation of its **Morris & Co.** windows. The five figures now to be seen in its east window together with the minstrel angels above were originally in the west window beneath the tower. There the figures of *St Martin, St Veronica, Christ as Love, St Agnes* and *St George* were accompanied by *St Peter,* the *Virgin Mary* and *St. Paul* the last three figures now being found in another window in the building. Before relocation the figures were shown in two tiers of four against blue drapery backgrounds with foliage and sky above and in the tracery six minstrel angels with various instruments (five now appearing in the east window). All the larger figures are **Burne-Jones** designs previously used in other locations (*St Agnes* is based on his design for the figure of *Humility*) with the minstrel angels coming from the pen of **William Morris.** The west window was installed in 1903.
Elsewhere in the south transept is St Catherine's chapel where there is an

undisturbed **Morris** window dating from ten years later. This depicts *St Elizabeth, St Edward* and *St Anne* on the upper tier with *St Aldhelm, St Catherine* and *St Osmund* beneath. The setting for the figures, with its blue background, foliage and sky, gives some idea of how the west window in the church would have appeared. All the figures are by **Burne-Jones** with the exception *St Catherine* that being by **Morris**. All the designs had been used before even when adapted from different figures. An example of this being how *St Edward* was based on a design for *King Alfred* this adapted figure first seeing the light of day at Morton in 1896.

Also of interest at St George's is a window of that saint on the south side of the chancel signed by its designer William Glasby and dating from the 1920s.

The church is open most days.

MAX GATE is signposted from the southern side of the Dorchester bypass a short distance down the A352 Wareham road.

MORRIS & CO.GLASS AT FORDINGTON. PHOTO BY BRIAN WISE

Hardy designed the house himself and lived in it from 1885 until his death in 1928. In the dining room is a portrait of Agatha Thornycroft who was one of the inspirations for the fictional character of *Tess*. The portrait was painted by Theodore Blake Wirgman (1848-1925) an artist who trained at the Royal Academy and knew **Walter Crane** professionally. Agatha was the wife of Hamo Thornycroft the sculptor, associated with the New Sculpture movement from the 1880s. Hardy had learnt stone carving from his father and Thornycroft later gave him a set of chisels. Most of the pet gravestones to be found in the garden of Max Gate were carved by Hardy himself.

Hardy knew a number of Pre-Raphaelite artists although none of them visited him at Max Gate. He would have met **Edward Burne-Jones** through their common membership of the Athenaeum Club in London although the artist is unlikely to have read a book such as *Tess of the D'Urbervilles* because of his dislike for a sad ending.

One man who did visit the house on many occasions from 1911 was Sydney Cockerell the director of the Fitzwilliam Museum in Cambridge and someone who had been friends with **William Morris** and **John Ruskin** earlier in his life. He was the former's assistant for a number of years and also much involved with the Kelmscott Press. Cockerell became a great friend of Hardy's too.

T.E. Lawrence (Lawrence of Arabia) amongst many other famous names visited as well- again he and Hardy were friends and it was Lawrence who knew the sculptor Kennington who completed a statue of Hardy after his death.

Max Gate is a National Trust property. It is open from the beginning of April until the end of October from Wednesday to Sunday 11-5.

MAX GATE. PHOTO BY KIND PERMISSION BY THE NATIONAL TRUST

FLEET is near Weymouth and signposted from the B3157 to the east of the town.

Moonfleet Manor Hotel (previously Fleet House) is an eighteenth century building with some internal work by **Lutyens** dating from the early nineteen-thirties.

The house is a hotel.

GILLINGHAM is in the very far north of the county.

The CHURCH OF ST MARY THE VIRGIN dates from the fourteenth century but has had further work completed in 1838-9 and 1908-9. Later in 1921 **W. D. Caroe** designed the south chapel.

The church may be locked but access is possible through the church wardens.

GUSSAGE ST. MICHAEL is located eight miles to the north-east of Blandford Forum off the A354.

The CHURCH OF ST. MICHAEL AND ALL ANGELS is entered through its north porch. Although its nave is largely thirteenth century the chancel was completely rebuilt by **G.E. Street** in about 1857. Of interest within it is the reredos dating from approximately 1870 and to be found behind the altar. Although the architectural historian Nikolaus Pevsner found its shapes to be *'ponderous'* the panels of stone and marble on the reredos are typical of **Street's** work at this time. The foliage that appears throughout the work is of fine quality. There is an inscription beneath in memory of George Dewdrey a rector in the parish and his wife Penelope both of whom died in 1869. When looking at the reredos it is worth remembering that it benefits from as much illumination as possible.

On either side of the reredos are a pair of rather Pre-Raphaelite angels painted on board. Nearby is the chancel screen is by C.E. Ponting (1919) which has some fine

DETAIL OF THE REREDOS IN THE CHURCH AT GUSSAGE ST. MICHAEL

carving particularly in its central section.

The church is open most days.

HIGHCLIFFE is about four miles to the east of Christchurch off the A337.

HIGHCLIFFE CASTLE (signposted from the A337) was built between 1831 and 1835 by Lord Stuart De Rothesay in the Picturesque style. The architect was William John Donthorn and the building was designed to include a huge library to house Stuart's enormous collection of books and manuscripts. The house was the second on the site the first being erected in 1770 and entitled High Cliff but demolished as its foundations had been seriously undermined by landslips. Lord Stuart De Rothesay was the son of the man responsible for the reluctant demolition General Charles Stuart whose own father was the Third Earl of Bute. It was the Earl who commissioned Robert Adam to design the first house as a country retreat.

Lord Stuart De Rothesay (the title was created in 1828 when he received a peerage) had a distinguished but occasionally controversial diplomatic career. He married Lady Elizabeth Yorke in 1816 and had two daughters Charlotte (later Countess Canning) and Louisa (later Marchioness of Waterford) and it is primarily Louisa who came into contact with members of the Pre-Raphaelite circle in the 1860s. Louisa (1818-91) and her sister were both very attractive girls who were also endowed with artistic talent. They both developed extensive skills in watercolour and Louisa had a fine contralto voice. Charlotte (1817-61) was probably not quite the equal of her sister as an artist but was highly intelligent with a good sense of humour. She married in 1835 and seven years later she became a lady-in-waiting to Queen Victoria a post she held for thirteen years. Whilst there, she had painting lessons from J.D. Harding and W.L. Leitch amongst other artists with her main subject matter being landscapes and buildings. Her husband Carlo (Viscount Charles Canning) was appointed Governor-General of India in 1855 and

Charlotte duly arrived at Calcutta with her husband at the beginning of the next year just two years before the Mutiny. She continued to paint and when **John Ruskin** saw some of her flower paintings completed in India he was much impressed. Charlotte was to spend the rest of her life on the sub-continent where she died in 1861 of malaria her husband dying less than a year later.

Louisa led a different kind of life. In 1836 her parents took her to Italy for six months where she studied the works of the Venetian Masters of the sixteenth century amongst others. Rather surprisingly in 1842 she married Lord Waterford a man with a reputation at the time for high and wild living. Despite this the marriage was a happy if childless one with the couple living at Curraghmore a vast estate in southern Ireland. Once there Louisa instigated a number of philanthropic initiatives designed to make the estate workers' lives easier. She was also a very religious person who to begin with supported the ideas of the Oxford Movement and although she later came to prefer a more low church form of service, her faith remained important throughout her life. She designed stained glass for her local church in Ireland and also produced glass for a window in Highcliffe church (this is no longer in evidence but examples of Louisa's fine art can be seen inside the church).

Her watercolours started to be more and more appreciated by established artists of the day including G.F. Watts who completed a portrait of Louisa in 1848. It was five years later that she was introduced to **John Ruskin** with whom she maintained a contact until the 1870s although this was mainly for professional advice rather than just out of friendship. One of the art critic's suggestions was that Louisa should seek tuition from **Rossetti.** His advice changed little during this time the main tenets of which were the importance of:

Accurate drawing
Study of the human figure
Observation of light and shade
Benefit of faithfulness to colour

The same year (1853) it was arranged for Louisa and her sister to view **Holman Hunt's** *Light of the World* in his studio at 5 Prospect Place in Cheyne Walk. Hunt described the scene in his book Pre-Raphaelitism and the Pre-Raphaelite Brotherhood-*'…one morning the sound of a carriage wheels stopped at the side entrance of my studio at Chelsea, and a loud knocking was followed by the names of the Marchioness of Waterford and Lady Canning. I received the ladies as they ascended to my studio saying that Mr Ruskin had assured them that they might call to see my picture'.*

The following February **Millais** planned to start a sketching club with eighteen members to include **Madox Brown, Rossetti, Hunt** and others with Lady Waterford also on the list. In the end the idea did not materialise but Louisa continued to take an avid interest in the work of the Pre-Raphaelites.

In July 1855 **Rossetti** wrote to his mother to tell her, *'An astounding event is to come off tomorrow. The Marchioness of Waterford has expressed a wish to Ruskin to see me paint in water-colour… She is herself an excellent artist and would have been really great, I believe, if not born such a swell and such a stunner… whether I shall be able to paint at all under the circumstances I have my doubts.'* The visit appears to have been helpful to Louisa as soon after she asked **Rossetti** to tutor her but he declined.

At the start of 1858 Louisa was instrumental in introducing **Ruskin** to Maria La Touche and subsequently the critic met her daughter Rose then aged nine and a girl destined to be disastrously involved with him in the next few years.

Tragically for Louisa her husband was killed in a hunting accident in 1859 and her life was abruptly changed. She had the additional grief of having to leave her home in Ireland as it became the property of a younger brother in her husband's family. Fortunately she was provided for by her deceased husband in the form of Ford Castle in Northumberland. Here she found she had more time to pursue her art and in particular drawing. Alas her beloved sister died in India only two years after from the effects of a fever and Louisa and her mother found themselves increasingly drawn together. Widowed in 1845 her mother had been living at Highcliffe and Louisa now divided her time between there and Ford usually preferring to spend the summer months in the south. In the same year of 1861 she began what is probably her most ambitious artwork in the form of a number of murals with biblical subjects at the village hall in Ford. In May she bumped into **Millais** at a dinner - in a letter to Effie his wife, he wrote, *'She is rather handsomer than when I saw her seven years ago-a little stouter, and certainly the noblest looking woman I ever saw'*. One hopes Effie took this remark in good stead particularly as a few days later he arranged to see Louisa again to look at some of her drawings-he wrote, *' She was so pleased, I think, for I found her drawings magnificent, so I could praise honestly. She was very kind and nice, and begged particularly to be remembered to you'*.

In a letter to Louisa of December 1863 **Ruskin** mentions to her that he knows that Rose La Touche is ill and wishes he did not care. She had suffered her first experience of mental illness which she was slow to recover from. Nearly three years later he himself was depressed as Rose's parents had denied him permission to write to or see her. This is the period of time when he found himself increasingly besotted by Rose and proposed marriage to her an offer that he repeated when she later came of age.

Sadly, Louisa's mother died in 1867 and she continued thereafter to spend her time between her two homes, Highcliffe and Ford. She met **Rossetti** once more in 1868 at Penkill Castle in Ayrshire where he was staying with William Bell Scott and his companion Alice Boyd. She would have discussed the illustrations of Christina Rossetti's poem *Maiden Song* that she was then working on and she might also have been interested in the mural that Bell Scott was completing on the castle staircase.

There is a rare mention of Highcliffe in a letter from **Ruskin** in January 1870 when he writes to her, *'What a tease it is your being away at that wild place-instead of at Verona or Venice - and at places tumbling into the sea over cliffs too'*. This is of course a reference to the landslides that created such a problem for buildings in the area.

Almost three years later the correspondence again reflects the traumatic circumstances of Rose La Touche's life when **Ruskin** writes that he cannot discuss religious pictures of any kind-this was connected to Rose having had another major mental breakdown this time accompanied by an obsessive religious mania. Louisa may well have written another sympathetic note when Rose died in May 1875 a period during which **Ruskin** described himself as *'utterly downcast'*. Her death is often seen as the trigger for his later poor mental health and own bouts of insanity.

Louisa's artistic career was enhanced at this point by her contact with her second cousin Coutts Lindsay who was the director of the emerging and increasingly popular Grosvenor Gallery an alternative hanging space to the ever conservative Royal Academy. Louisa showed her pictures there every year from 1878 to 1882. She also exhibited at the Dudley gallery another new exhibiting space in 1887 when her submitted water-colour was mistakenly thought to be the work of a man and subsequently praised highly by a critic. This was unlikely to have happened had she been identified correctly as the artist.

Highcliffe was visited by members of the Royal Family in 1880, 1881 and also in 1885 and on each occasion the party was headed by the Prince and Princess of Wales

STATUE OF LOUISA WATERFORD BY J.E. BOEHM AT HIGHCLIFFE

using the royal yacht to make the trip from Osborne House on the Isle of Wight. Louisa visited Osborne in the summer of 1890 when she was aged seventy-two and during her stay Queen Victoria viewed a number of her drawings including one she particularly liked by the title of *Relentless Time* which Louisa then insisted she should have.

Louisa died only a year later at Ford and subsequently a memorial exhibition of her work was held in London which was attended by both G.F Watts and Henry James who were both impressed by the standard of pictures shown. Watts and his wife Mary Seton Watts designed her gravestone which can be found at the Church of St. Michael in Ford.

Highcliffe is now open to the public having been fully restored following a fire in 1967. It is open most days from 11-5 from the beginning of February until just before Xmas.

The CHURCH OF ST MARK in the village of Highcliffe was erected in 1842 through land and finance supplied by Charles, Lord Stuart De Rothsay. The architect of the original building was a local man John Bemister and there were subsequent additions completed by Benjamin Ferrey. The building contains some artworks by Louisa, Marchioness of Waterford who was in contact with a number of personalities associated with Pre-Raphaelitism throughout her life (see section on Highcliffe Castle). The original east window is thought to have been designed by her

HIGHCLIFFE CASTLE

but this was later destroyed to be replaced with glass by **James Powell & Sons.** Still to be seen however is an oil painting whose subject is the *Sleeping Disciples* another version of which is in the Tate collection. Also to be found in the church office is a watercolour by Louisa with the title *Suffer the Little Children*. Louisa greatly admired the fifteenth century Italian painter Antonella da Messina and she copied a picture by him showing *Christ with the Virgin Mary and St John* which can be found in the clergy vestry.

Louisa and her sister Charlotte met **William Holman Hunt** during their lifetime at the time that he was painting *The Light of the World* so it does seem appropriate there is a print of the same work to be found near the font.

There are also some good examples of stained glass to be seen within the church. On the north wall of the nave is glass by **Clayton & Bell** dating from around 1901 and in the east wall of the north transept an example of **H T Bosdet's** work depicting the archangels *Gabriel* and *Michael*.

Lord Stuart De Rothsay died in 1845 and his memorial tablet can be found in the chancel. There also tablets to the memory of Louisa and Charlotte.

The church may be locked but access is possible through the church wardens.

HINTON MARTELL is located off the B3078 some five miles to the north of Wimborne Minster.

GAUNT HOUSE has a brick house and stables by **George Devey.**
Used as a retreat and as a vocational centre.

IWERNE COURTNEY or SHROTON is found six miles to the north-west of Blandford Forum along the A350.

There is one feature of the CHURCH OF ST MARY which is reason enough to find the key-holder, should the building to be locked. Inside there is a rare reredos made of terracotta dating from 1889. Surprisingly this was designed by a local aristocrat in her own pottery. The woman in question is Amia S. (Lady) Baker who lived at Ranston an eighteenth century house a quarter of a mile to the south-east. This amazing reredos has beautifully rendered grapes, vine leaves and corn ears, set amongst figures of angels and a bust of Christ. It is the sort of naturalistic work of which the Pre-Raphaelites would have approved particularly in their early years. It is inscribed on the rear and the whole design is very charming with its miniature ceramic columns. It is rumoured locally that Doultons may have supplied the terracotta clay.

One other item in the church may be of interest to visitors from the United States but is far more ancient than the Pre-Raphaelites or Arts and Crafts movement. This is in the Freke chapel in the northern corner of the church. The heraldic shield here could be seen as a precursor to the Stars and Stripes.

The church may be locked but access is possible through the church wardens.

IWERNE MINSTER is seven miles to the north of Blandford Forum on the A350.

This village has a number of features either loosely of more closely connected to the art of the Pre-Raphaelites and their stylistic descendants. As you turn off the A350 into the village you will most likely see Giles Gilbert Scott's graceful war memorial dating from 1919 and shortly afterwards a stone shelter erected about the same time with a lively figure of Mercury on its pediment. Both have qualities associated with the Arts and Crafts movement with the latter being erected by James Ismay who was a great benefactor to the village at this time. He had purchased the estate of the Wolvertons in 1908 (now the Clayesmore School) where the architect Alfred Waterhouse had built a large and rambling house in 1878 (to be seen on the other side of the A350). Another

REREDOS IN THE CHURCH AT IWERNE COURTNEY

DETAIL OF WHALL WINDOW AT IWERNE MINSTER

architect Baillie Scott designed a hall for the village in 1921 in an Arts and Crafts manner and this can still be seen close to the church although now it is a private house.

The CHURCH OF ST MARY continues the theme magnificently in the form of its five lighted east window. This is another **Christopher Whall** window in the county and a particularly fine one. The flowing design is redolent of the artist at the height of his powers with a stunning use of contrasting clear and coloured glass. It dates from 1920.

In addition there is good glass by **James Powell & Sons** in both the north and south chapels. The expensive south chapel with its exquisite vaulted roof was added to the church by **J.L. Pearson** in 1889.

Lastly, but by no means least, are the two mosaic panels in the south aisle depicting *Boaz* (who befriended Ruth) and *St George*. These two large and impressive examples of the genre were probably executed by **Powells**.

The church is open most days.

MOSAIC PANEL OF ST GEORGE AT IWERNE MINSTER

KIMMERIDGE is about ten miles west of Swanage along the A351 to Corfe Castle and then down an unclassified road.

The modest CHURCH OF ST NICHOLAS was largely constructed in 1872 although the south doorway is mainly Norman. Inside there are a number of equally modest memorials to the past inhabitants of Smedmore, a house a mile to the south-east. One of these later families, the Mansels is commemorated in the east window designed by **C.E. Kempe** (his wheatsheaf is on the left-hand side). This glass was installed in 1904 and has as its subject the *Appearance to St Mary Magdalene by Christ,* the same design as that to be found in the church at West Lulworth. The inscription around the window *Holy Holy Holy Lord God Almighty* probably dates from a similar time. Today the glass is the main focal point of the interior.

The church is open most days.

KIMMERIDGE

KINGSTON lies about five miles east of Swanage along the B3069

The CHURCH OF ST. JAMES was built between the years 1873-80 and replaced an older building (only by about forty years) that for a considerable while afterwards served as the church hall. The builder of the new church was **George Edmund Street** who was commissioned to build it by the 3rd Earl of Eldon. It is certainly an imposing edifice with great height the tower being visible for miles around. The church has been called **Street's** finest in the country and there is expensive quality to be seen throughout although some writers have commented that it lacks passion.

It does contain very beautiful examples of ironwork designed by the architect that contribute to the largely monochrome textures of the interior which has the feel of a cathedral. The stained glass is all by **Clayton & Bell.**

St James's was one of the last churches to be completed by **Street** many years after his offices were a leading light in the development of the Arts and Crafts movement with **Morris** and **Webb** working under him. He died in 1881 aged only fifty-seven.

The church may be locked but access is possible through the church wardens.

LONG BREDY is north-west of Abbotsbury along an unclassified road off the B3157.

Ashley Chase is a house built in the **Lutyens** style by **Edward Guy Dawber** in 1925. It was originally intended to be a shooting lodge.

The house is private.

LYME REGIS is a coastal town in the extreme west of the county.

The CHURCH OF ST MICHAEL THE ARCHANGEL is a striking turreted building in an equally striking location being at its nearest point only twenty yards from the sea.

Once inside the statue of an angel with two trumpets appears like a three dimensional version of a **Burne-Jones** design for stained glass. The actual glass herein is also of some interest, beginning with the window depicting *Sir Galahad and the Holy Grail* on the north wall of the nave. Although the designer is uncertain the subject is one that was very popular especially with the second wave of Pre-Raphaelite artists and designers that included **Burne-Jones** as well as **William Morris** and **Walter Crane.** The design in this case seems however to be at least partly based on a G.F. Watts painting *Sir Galahad with a Horse* (third panel from the left) that has also been used elsewhere in the country in tiling and stained glass work. Opposite on the south side of the nave is a memorial window by **James Powell & Sons** which according to a descriptive sign nearby was designed by E.B. Powell in 1921. In addition to the figures of *St Michael, St George, St Nicholas* and *St Gabriel* the design also incorporates a local

DETAIL OF POWELL & SONS WINDOW AT LYME REGIS

SUNDIAL HOUSE (LEFT) IN LYME REGIS

scene featuring The Cobb. There is further glass by **James Powell & Sons** in the north-east corner of the church and a window by **C.E. Kempe & Co. Ltd.** of 1913 showing another St Michael can be seen on the north side of the tower.

The church is open most days.

SUNDIAL HOUSE (on Marine Parade) was built by the architect **Arnold Mitchell** after he retired and came to live in Lyme in the nineteen-twenties. It is a distinctive shape which means it has few rooms but many stairs making it a home that is unusual to live in, but one with spectacular views. The five storey house is constructed of local limestone rubble with a façade dominated by a series of bay windows beneath a separate hooded roof; the sundial after which the house is named can be seen below the leaded light windows of the third floor. The building remains a late Arts and Crafts delight.

The house is private.

The latter day Pre-Raphaelite painter **John Byam Shaw** spent time in the area during the summer of 1893 preparing studies for his early work *The Blessed Damozel* based on **Rossetti's** poem of the same name.

MARNHULL is just over ten miles east of Sherborne via the A30 and Landshire Lane.

The principal reason for visiting the CHURCH OF ST GREGORY is to view the main east window produced by **Morris & Co.** in 1911. It shows from left to right; the *Virgin Mary, Christ on the Cross* and *St John.* In the lights above the figures of *Mary* and

John are *Angels with the Sun* and *with the Moon.* In the quatrefoils further above are three-quarter length *Angels with Harps* and a *Dove descending* at the very top. All these designs are by **Burne-Jones,** the three main figures first being used at St Michael and All Angels church in Torquay in 1878. They were also used in a similar composition with the angels above and in the same panel at Allerton, Liverpool in 1885. At the bottom of the window a reredos with a tiled picture of *The Good Shepherd* partly obscures the glass making it difficult to see if the window has an inscription.

On the north wall of the chancel there is an interesting signed window of 1897 from the studios of William George Taylor (who went into partnership with another glassmaker William Henry O'Connor in 1873 and later headed up his own firm) and elsewhere in the building are windows by Alexander Gibbs. To some degree the Taylor window suggests the influence of **Morris & Co.** at the time but none of the windows do much to

MORRIS & CO WINDOW IN MARNHULL CHURCH

dismiss the idea that the interior of this church is a little on the austere side.

The village of Marlot in Hardy's *Tess of the D'Urbervilles* was based on Marnhull. *The church is open most days.*

MELPLASH is two and a half miles to the south of Beaminster straight down the A3066.

CHRIST CHURCH is a large imposing neo-Norman building constructed in 1845-6 for a then perceived increase in the local population (and therefore in the local congregation) as a result of changing cottage industry trends. In fact a flax industry to serve the Bridport rope and net market never really came about and the initiative to fund the building of the church by James Bandinel, a local landowner was ill-founded. The church was designed by Benjamin Ferrey (1810-80) who had studied architecture with **Pugin** in his younger days. Later in his life he would publish a book about these experiences under the title of *Recollections of A.W.N. Pugin and has father Augustus Pugin*. Christ Church is however far removed from his mentor's sense of ecclesiastical style and is based on an original Norman church in Shoreham, Sussex. Seen from the road it is a truly imposing edifice sitting as it does adjacent to the school also built by James Bandinel.

Entry is now made through a door at the end of the south transept where a plaque commemorates the intentions of Bandinel. The reason for entering the building through this door almost immediately becomes apparent. The nave now has a glazed screen across it dividing it into two. Since 1975 the body of the nave has been empty of permanent fittings and used for meetings and functions but is presently decked out as a badminton court. The remainder of the building is still used for services with the south transept now forming a new nave and the north transept a sanctuary. The impressive former

FORMER SANCTUARY AT MELPLASH

apsidal sanctuary has become a roomy baptistery. Perhaps surprisingly, it all appears to work and function, even if the sight of the former nave is initially rather shocking.

The former sanctuary has attractive tiled floor and walls and a decorated ceiling and there are rounded single lancets of stained glass. The honest wooden pulpit has been moved but only marginally and now occupies a position convenient to the new arrangement. The church appears to have been an expensive project and one which proved unnecessary but as a building it is a convincing one.

The church is open most days.

MILTON ABBEY is twelve miles to the north-east of Dorchester signposted from the A354.

The ABBEY CHURCH was restored from its then ruinous state by **Sir George Gilbert Scott** in 1865. In the south transept is the large Jesse window of seven lights designed by **Augustus Pugin** in 1847 and made by **John Hardman.** It can be seen from the great man's diary that he travelled down from Dorcester to Milton Abbey on the 30th September 1847 and left a day later. It may have been the intention to have a series of windows designed by **Pugin** but in the event only one was realised.

The church is used by the adjacent school but the building is often open.

MILTON

MINTERNE MAGNA is just over ten miles north of Dorchester on the A352.

MINTERNE HOUSE was built in 1904-6 by **Leonard Stokes** an architect working within the Art and Crafts movement but here using an abundance of styles in order to find one of his own. It was designed for the Digby family who are related to another illustrious family the Churchills (of Winston fame) and both families have memorials in the church nearby. The house is constructed of Ham Hill ashlar which gives the exterior a wonderful warm appearance and adopts amongst attributes of many styles, a Gothic side (the north) and an Elizabethan one (the south). The eye is constantly stimulated as one circles the house with its mixture of pediments, battlements, leadlight windows and use of perpendicular and semi-circular motifs. **Stokes** was the brother of the artist Adrian Stokes(1854-1935) who studied at the Royal Academy in 1872-5 and was a painter of landscape, portraits and genre. In 1884 he married the Austrian artist Marianne Preindlsberger who exhibited with him and also separately under her married name. She completed works in a style similar to Arthur Gaskin and Joseph Southall and other Birmingham artists of the time influenced by the Pre-Raphaelites.

W. A. S. Benson appears to have also possibly designed a house here at Minterne as there are entries in his wife's diaries to this effect but it is not known which if any buildings transpired as a result.

The accompanying garden at Minterne is also a delight particularly by the river and when the Himalayan rhododendrons are in bloom.

Minterne Gardens are open daily to the public from March-November 10am-6pm.

MINTERNE MAGNA HOUSE

MONKTON WYLD is to be found four miles north of Lyme Regis via the A3052 and the A35 from which it is signposted.

Richard Cromwell Carpenter built the CHURCH OF ST ANDREW in 1848-9 to a Gothic design. He was a supporter of the Cambridge Camden Society who advocated a return to medieval ritual in church services as well as a church plan and appearance based on Gothic correctness. The Society had been formed in 1839 and changed its name to the Ecclesiastical Society when it moved its base to London in 1845. **Ruskin** and the Pre-Raphaelites largely agreed with the aims of the Society which was very influential at the time this church was built. Inside the building is a typically long chancel and many other features aligned to Ecclesiastical principles. There are in addition five fine stained glass windows with figures set against dense foliage made by **George Edward**

Cook (date uncertain). He was probably also the designer but whatever the case the stained glass here is a triumph.

The church may be locked but access is possible through the church wardens.

The centre of POOLE lies less than six miles west of Bournemouth.

ALL SAINTS CHURCH is found in Western Road in the Branksome Park area of Poole. It was built by the architectural partnership of Burton & Stevens in 1877 and has a decorated polygonal eastern apse. There were also windows in the building by **C.E. Kempe & Co. Ltd.** at the western end. These dated from 1925 with two lights showing *St Elizabeth* and *John the Baptist* and in the same vicinity a three lighted window from three years earlier with the figures of the saints *Michael Gabriel* and *Raphael.* Unfortunately, these windows now only contain clear glass and the whereabouts of the **Kempe** glass is unknown. The windows here were made well after the death of **Charles Eamer Kempe** in 1907.

Outside in the graveyard to the north of the church and near to the road, is a wonderful granite cross with an Art Nouveau bronze in memory of James Simpson who died in 1917. This marvellously emotive work was designed by Crossland McClure who was also responsible for three figures with a musical theme in the Usher Hall in Edinburgh.

The church may on occasion be locked but access is possible through the church wardens.

ART NOUVEAU CROSS IN THE GRAVEYARD AT ALL SAINTS POOLE

ST LUKE'S CHURCH is in Sandecotes Road Parkstone.

The architect was J. Henry Ball (1861-1931) in conjunction with a local man T.J.B. Holland. The building was completed 1907-8. Ball also did St Agatha's church in Portsmouth which was more inspired in the form of an Early English basilica with decoration inside by Heywood Sumner. Ball was a pupil of Alfred Waterhouse who practised in Southsea until 1896 later moving to London.

The church is open most days.

ST. PETER'S CHURCH is in Church Road Parkstone.

The present church is the second on the site and the foundation stone for it was laid in August 1876. The initial parts of the building were completed to the plans of Frederick Rogers and these included the chancel and transepts. Much of the rest of the church as we see it today was to the designs of **John Loughborough Pearson** and later his son F.L. (Frank) Pearson and by 1901 everything major except a proposed spire had been completed. This was however never constructed due to a late withdrawal of funding-an amount of some 10000 pounds going instead towards the building costs of nearby St Luke's church. No doubt **J.L. Pearson's** work here was not controversial as when later he was asked to do restoration work at Peterborough cathedral in 1896 and came up against the Society for the Protection of Ancient Buildings (SPAB). This confrontation followed on from another-in 1885 **Morris** and other members of SPAB objected to **Pearson's** plans for a two storeyed cloister range to be incorporated into the older fabric of Westminster Hall.

The style of St. Peter's is a mix of Early English and Early French architectural tastes and impresses the viewer both externally and internally by sheer scale. Within this marvellous space are a number of interesting features. One of the most obvious is the rood screen of wrought iron designed by **Pearson Snr.** and installed at about the time that he was first engaged in working on the building (1877). The font (and cover) as well as the pulpit are by his son and can be found relatively close-by dating from 1907 and 1909 respectively. The stained glass in the Chapel of the Holy Name (to the south-

INTERIOR OF ST PETER'S CHURCH POOLE

east) is instantly identifiable as being by **Kempe.** The two long lancets show *Saint Elizabeth of Hungary* and *Saint Margaret of Scotland.* They were installed in 1904 and the company logo of a single wheatsheaf can be seen. Also of interest and nearer the west window is a fine framed embroidery showing *St. Osmund* which is one of two such works to be found in the church. The carved foliate capitals that appear throughout the nave are also wonderful. The tiled floors that make such an impact in this space were installed by **Carter & Co.** of Poole in 1877.

Lastly, and in a particularly Pre-Raphaelite vein, is the stained glass window in the south wall of the nave depicting a fairly faithful copy of **Holman Hunt's** ubiquitous painting *The Light of the World.*

The church is often open but if locked access is possible through the church wardens.

STAINED GLASS INSPIRED BY "THE LIGHT OF THE WORLD" IN ST. PETER'S CHURCH POOLE

The EX-CHURCH OF ST. OSMUND (NOW CHURCH OF ST. STEPHEN GREAT ORTHODOX CHRISTIAN CHURCH) is in Bournemouth Road Parkstone.

This church was **E. S. Prior's** last major work and was designed with Arthur Grove (1870-1929). Grove collaborated with **Prior** on many occasions and was in the office of **J. D. Sedding** and also worked with **Henry Wilson.** The church dates from 1913-16 and had to incorporate an earlier brick structure in the Byzantine style by local architect G.A.B. Livesay built about ten years earlier. The exterior in particular is exuberant but at the same time strange. There are the subdued colours of the specially commissioned bricks presented as they are in a variety of patterns. The bricks were produced by a pottery near Wareham and range in colour from brown to yellow to purple to red. The west end of the building is quite a hybrid with its two galleries and rose window consisting of two concentric circles topped by two exotic turrets. The interior is mainly roughcast but with terracotta detailing found for example, in the figures of angels in the Byzantine column capitals. All the terracotta was supplied by **Carter & Co.** of Poole. There are also abundant examples of **Prior's** typically thick stained glass in abstract designs. The church has other items of interest within its spacious Arts and Crafts interior including sculptures and a painting of the *Annunciation* by MacDonald Gill, brother of Eric. **Eric Gill** is represented by the inscriptions on the altar of the Incarnation Chapel.

The hand beaten bronze lectern by W. Bainbridge Reynolds is wonderful the same designer contributing an altar cross and candelabras *(the author has been unable to verify whether the work by Bainbridge Reynolds is still in the church at time of writing)*. The church was declared redundant in 2002 and there have been further administrative problems during its life as the Church of St. Stephen.

The church may be locked so it could be prudent to phone before planning to visit.
HOLY ANGELS CHURCH is in Lilliput Road Parkstone

The exterior of this building was criticized rather emphatically by Nikolaus Pevsner as *'a horrid chapel in buff brick'* but even if this is conceded as being partly correct the interior does much to compensate. The church nave was begun in 1874 with the chancel and two aisles being added later. In the now much changed interior is a rood screen by **G.F. Bodley** in addition to choir stalls and a stencilled organ case by the same man. The latter has been retained despite the church now using an electric organ. All these fitments are decorated some with text and perhaps over-painted.

The main attraction is undoubtedly the triptych bas-relief in a wooden frame to be seen on the north wall. This depicts a *Pieta* in white marble in the central panel with silver coloured angels to either side.

It is by **Arthur George Walker** and signed by the artist being very much in an Art Nouveau style. The sculpture used to be on a more southerly wall before an extension was built in the north-west corner of the church. It is a charming combination of forms but just how it came to its present location is somewhat of a mystery. It is known however that

SCULPTURAL RELIEF BY A. G. WALKER IN HOLY ANGELS POOLE

although **Walker** was London based for much of his life he had an address in Dorset after 1933. The putti depicted above the main piece may have been more recently painted.

The church is usually locked but access is possible through the church wardens.

ST. ANNE'S HOSPITAL is in Haven Road, Canford Cliffs.

This imposing red brick building was constructed in 1909-12 and is by the Scottish architect **Robert Weir Schultz** in partnership with **F.R. Troup.** In this particular building they achieved one that combined functionality with aesthetic concerns. Hence we see a hospital with rooms offering great views and light filled corridors all to aid the recuperation of its patients. The outside has a satisfying appearance with its shaped gables, unostentatious brickwork and stone dressings.

Private building.

PRESTON is three and a half miles to the east from Weymouth along the A353.

The CHURCH OF ST. ANDREW was extensively restored or perhaps over-restored by T.H. Wyatt in 1855. Wyatt came from a family of architects and appears to have gained a bit of a reputation for insensitive work although his rebuilding of Tarrant Gunville seems less controversial than here.

The church interior has an encaustic tiled pavement in the chancel probably dating from the time of the restoration. In addition there is a window by **C.E. Kempe & Co. Ltd.** under the tower at the west end of the building. This shows *St Margaret Virgin and Martyr* on the left and the figure of *St. Margaret of Scotland* adjacent. The window of two lights with quatrefoil above dates from 1908 and has the studio's logo of the period-a wheatsheaf with black tower superimposed at the lower left-hand side. This makes this **Kempe** window contemporary with that at Tarrant Gunville.

Another window worthy of attention in this somewhat bare setting is that

KEMPE WINDOW IN PRESTON CHURCH

commemorating Constance Conway and found in the south wall of the chancel. She was much involved with the parish during her lifetime and this window is charming with its detailed depictions of flora and fauna.

The church may be locked but access is possible through the church wardens.

PURSE CAUNDLE is four and a half miles to the east of Sherborne along the A30.

CRENDLE COURT (on the northern side of the A30) is the work of **Walter Henry Brierley.** The house is banded on its exterior walls and use is made of local ashlar and stone.

Private house.

RAMPISHAM is about seven and a half miles to the east of Beaminster along the B3163 and the A356.

The CHURCH OF ST MICHAEL was restored in 1845-7 when its chancel was completed by **A.W.N. Pugin.** He also designed the east window which was completed by **Hardman.** In the village the rectory was one of only three houses he designed for middle class clients.

The church is locked on occasion.

SHERBORNE is in the north-west corner of the county close to Yeovil.

SHERBORNE ABBEY must be a highlight amongst ecclesiastical buildings in Dorset. It is such a beautiful and elegant building one can initially be overwhelmed by all it offers. Of particular munificence is the fan vaulting probably dating from the fifteenth century. Much later **W.D. Caroe** was responsible for the upper part of the screen in the Chapel of St. Mary le Bow and also modified the east end of the Lady Chapel. Here he installed very slim stone and wooden screens. **R.H. Carpenter** completed the reredos in the choir in 1884 with the figures in relief carved by James Forsyth. The same sculptor was responsible for the pulpit of 1899 although its design is by B. Ingelow who was **Carpenter's** partner. In regards to stained glass **Pugin** designed the *Te Deum* window in the south transept with its ninety-six figures and it was installed by **John Hardman** in about 1850-2. It has unfortunately not survived well and as with other glass in the Abbey it has faded badly due to the underfiring of the paint. There is in addition good **Clayton & Bell** glass to be found in

REREDOS AND WALL DECORATION AT SHERBORNE

the Great East window and the choir clerestory windows. The same firm completed the appealing decoration on the walls and vault hereabouts.

The abbey is open most days.

SHERBORNE SCHOOL FOR GIRLS (in Bradford Road) was designed by **Reginald Theodore Blomfield** in one of his later styles.

Private building.

SHERBORNE ABBEY

SHILLINGSTONE is five miles north-west of Blandford Forum along the A357.

The CHURCH OF THE HOLY ROOD has attractive ceiling decoration dating from its last restoration in 1902. There are also gilded bosses and beams high above in both the nave and chancel with the latter's decoration being of darker colour. The architect **G.F. Bodley,** completed the scheme about fifteen years after the church's previous restoration by F.W. Hunt, who added both the north aisle and arcade to the original largely Norman building.

The stained glass over the west door was designed and given by **Mary Lowndes** and her partner Barbara Forbes (1871-1946) in memory of Richard Forbes Lowndes who was killed in the Great War aged only nineteen. It is also dedicated to all the soldiers and sailors from the village that lost their lives in the conflict.

Lowndes was born locally and became an Art and Crafts designer (see section on Sturminster Newton) who in 1907 founded the Artists' Suffrage League mainly to give artistic support to the National Union of Women's Suffrage Societies. A number of professional artists got involved with the League whilst she was their chairperson and Forbes the secretary. Both women designed many banners and Christmas cards and other artefacts for the cause. When **Lowndes** died in 1929 she left money and all her artistic work to Forbes in her will. The church guide states that the late Eveline Tate (nee Bower)

DECORATED ROOF IN SHILLINGSTONE CHURCH

who lived at the nearby Church House was involved with Forbes in the design of the window. It also suggests that **Bodley's** decorative work may have replaced a painting by Alfred George Stephens who was actually primarily a sculptor and born at Blandford Forum.

The church is open most days.

SHROTON see IWERNE COURTNEY

STINSFORD is less than two miles north-east of Dorchester along the B3150.

The CHURCH OF ST. MICHAEL is mainly thirteenth century but was the recipient of a number of Victorian restorations. It was much loved by Thomas Hardy who would walk to it from his home at Max Gate about a mile away across the valley of the River Frome. The village of Mellstock that appears in his novels, is partly based on Stinsford.

Hardy's first wife Emma is buried here as well as other members of the family and although the great man's ashes were interred in Poets Corner at Westminster Abbey Hardy's heart literally lies here with her.

Inside the church in the south aisle is a memorial window to Hardy designed by Douglas Strachan (1875-1950) depicting *Elijah* in an Old Testament scene that was a favourite of the poet's. It was installed in 1930. Strachan was one of the most significant Scottish designers of stained glass of the twentieth century and was inspired by the work of **Christopher Whall.**

Outside and close by to Hardy's grave is the last resting place of Cecil Day-Lewis (1904-1972).

The church is open most days.

STOURPAINE is about three miles north-west of Blandford Forum along the A350.

HOLY TRINITY CHURCH consists of a fifteenth century tower and a nineteenth century remainder. This is due to the original structure being deemed to be so dilapidated in 1855 that all but the tower was swept away to be replaced by a chancel to the design of T.H. Wyatt and a nave one third longer in length. Wyatt performed a similar job at nearby Child Okeford.

The main item of interest inside the church is the tiles to be seen either side of the altar. These appear to date from the late nineteenth century and add much needed decoration to a plain wall. The tiles show in muted colours the four *Signs of the Evangelists* plus a *Lamb of God* on each side. There is a floral border between the subjects. They are not commented on in an otherwise comprehensive church guide which seems an oversight. The tiles have some of the style of **Walter Crane.**

Before leaving there are two other interesting pieces. On the north wall there is a nice coloured relief from the 1920's commemorating a former vicar and his wife.

There is also a copy of Raphael's *Madonna Della Sedia* in the nave which appears on the wall in the background to **Millais'** painting *Eliza Wyatt and her daughter, Sarah* of c.1850. It is used in the picture to highlight the differences between the angular early Pre-Raphaelite style and Raphael's rounded graceful forms-the latter exemplifying in its softened idealised way everything the Pre-Raphaelite Brotherhood was rebelling against.

There is one other indirect connection to the Brotherhood at Stourpaine, when the church was reconsecrated and rededicated in 1858, the service was conducted by Bishop Hamilton (Bishop of Salisbury) who supported the Oxford Movement. Also known as High Church this was a group of Anglicans who were in favour of having more aspects of Catholicism in their services principally seen in the use of more ritual. It has been suggested that some members of the Brotherhood and its associates were heavily

TILE DEPICTING THE SYMBOL FOR ST. MARK IN STOURPAINE CHURCH

influenced by some of the ideas mooted by these Tractarians (another name for its sympathisers). Even the notion of an all male Brotherhood was seen to be based on monkish principles. The church today has little in its simple appearance to connect it to the Oxford Movement.

When leaving the churchyard there is a fine example of a Victorian lych-gate made with dark wood that contrasts wonderfully with the stone of the church.

The church is occasionally locked but access is possible through the church wardens.

STUDLAND is close to the sea three and a half miles to the north of Swanage along the Ulwell road.

This CHURCH OF ST NICHOLAS is truly an ancient building being almost entirely Norman. The chancel arches in particular are exceptional being of a scale rarely seen elsewhere. Perhaps surprisingly (for there is little visual evidence) there was extensive restoration completed here between 1881-3 and it was this work that effectively saved the church from collapsing. **William Morris** would have been happy with the results and he was at least partly responsible for the sensitivity of the restoration. In 1877 he had with other concerned people including many connected to the Pre-Raphaelites founded the Society for the Protection of Ancient Buildings (SPAB) with a view to protect them from the overzealous restorations that were popular at the time. Their

STUDLAND CHURCH

stance was described as 'anti-scrape' which referred to their abhorrence of the practice of scrapping away the historical fabric of ancient buildings.

Here at Studland the SPAB's architect was Mr Vinall and he was responsible for finding out that the church was in such a precarious state and suggesting work such as underpinning and replastering in order to save it.

The church is open most days.

Also in the village is HILL CLOSE a house designed by **C.F.A. Voysey** in 1856 with his usual roughcast walls and mullioned windows except that in this case the windows are framed by blocks of the local Purbeck stone.

Private house.

STURMINSTER NEWTON is just over twelve miles east of Sherborne via the A3030 and A357.

The CHURCH OF ST. MARY is best known for its late fifteenth century wagon roof in the nave. The building had an expensive restoration in 1825 courtesy of Thomas Lane Fox who held the unusual position of being both wealthy patron of the church and its curate. It also has some wonderful and rare stained glass from the period of the Arts and Crafts movement.

This is by **Mary Lowndes** whose father was the vicar here for almost forty years. A window commemorating him can be found in the south chapel signed by his daughter and Isabel Lilian Gloag (c.1867-1917). Gloag seems to have worked with her regularly around 1900 and had previously studied at St John's Wood Art School and the Slade. She is known to have exhibited at the Royal Academy between 1893 and 1916 and her early work was in a Pre-Raphaelite style one of her pictures depicting Keats' *Isabella* a subject more famously painted by both **Millais** and **Holman Hunt.** She also produced a number of designs for banners to be used by societies and organisations allied to the suffragettes.

Another window by the artist in memory of her mother can be glimpsed above the entrance to the church in the west tower. Due to modernisation in the nave **Lowndes'** first ever window is difficult to see close up, but her use of colour can still be appreciated from a short distance. The main east window also has a family dedication although the designer here is **Hardman & Co.** of Birmingham.

Easily the most astounding and perhaps controversial window in the church is found to the south of the nave, this being a rare example in England of a design by **Harry Clarke.** He has been described as 'the last of the Pre-Raphaelites' although that title has been ascribed to a number of artist and designers. It was in 1919 that he submitted an initial drawing for a commission to design this window here in St. Mary's and this was accepted. The window shows *St Elizabeth of Hungary* (a thirteenth century queen) on the left with the *Madonna and Child* in the centre light. On the right is the figure of the third century martyr *St Barbara* whose features are based on those of his wife, Margaret. The glass was completed by 1921 and **Clarke** is reported as being (unusually) pleased with the results. Of particular note are the wonderfully colourful backdrops to the main figures with their non-specific geometric shapes. Beneath the window is an explanatory panel which indicates that the lower scene in the central light (showing the shepherds)

DETAIL OF WINDOW BY HARRY CLARKE AT STURMINSTER NEWTON

is set in landscape near St Alban's Head and on the Isle of Purbeck.

There is also glass by Geoffrey Webb in the north aisle of the church.
The church is open most days.

SIGNED WINDOW BY LOWNDES AND GLOAG AT STURMINSTER NEWTON

SUTTON WALDRON is eight miles north of Blandford Forum on the A350.

The CHURCH OF ST BARTHOLEMEW was built in 1847 and its main claim to fame today is that it contains probably the most important surviving decorative scheme by **Owen Jones.** In his writings he advocated his strong views on the use of colour and included illustrations of gilded columns which he considered a desirable form of decoration. This is one of his ideas used at Sutton Waldron and his use of abstract patterning is another. In the 1840's he developed an interest in tiling and mosaics sometimes in partnership with **Herbert Minton** and there are **Minton** tiles to be seen near the font and in the chancel although the latter tiles are likely to have been designed by **Pugin.**

Jones' designs were based on the idea that all ornament should be based on geometric principles and this can be seen clearly in this building where much precise use is also made of red yellow and blue, the same colours he used when asked to decorate the Great Exhibition of 1851.

The overall scheme at Sutton Waldron with its wood and stone carvings in addition to the use of biblical texts and exotic colours creates quite an impression to the visitor even on a dull day.

The church is usually open most days.

SWANAGE is on the coast in the south-east corner of the county.

In **Walter Crane's** autobiographical book *An Artist's Reminiscences* he mentions visiting Swanage with his wife and daughter Beatrice in the summer of 1874. He writes

PULPIT IN SUTTON WALDRON CHURCH

TILES AND ALTAR AT SUTTON WALDRON

that the town at that time was not connected to the main railway line and consequently they had a drive by coach of about eleven miles to get there. He also makes the comment that Swanage, *'was then a very charming primitive little village'*. It follows that by 1907 when the book was published he thought this was no longer the case.

His watercolour *An Orchard by a Stream* of 1874 (in the collection of The British Museum) may have been painted in the vicinity of Swanage.

Henry Holiday also came to Swanage and completed two paintings here. In the summer of 1857 he completed a landscape painting entitled *Durleston Bay*. This and a view of the town were shown at the Royal Academy the following year.

SWANAGE

SYMONDSBURY is less than two miles west of Bridport via the B3162.

The CHURCH OF ST JOHN THE BAPTIST is made of lovely warm local sandstone and sits in the centre of a charming village. On the opposite side of the road and complementing the church is the former Raymond's Charity School built in Victorian times from the same stone.

In this spot it is easy to imagine that things change slowly if at all but in fact the church has been the subject of two rather drastic restorations.

The first of these commenced in 1818 and would not be entirely completed until twenty years later. The results of all this labour included new box pews, a covering up of the barrel roof and two new galleries to accommodate the rising numbers of the congregation. However, all the changes were undone in the period 1920-6 when the roof was re-exposed, the galleries and box pews removed as well as all the plaster from the walls. In addition, the ironwork of the windows and other early nineteenth century modifications were taken down in a return to a more medieval church in a restoration that went in the face of the ethos behind so many Victorian restorations. The opportunity was however taken to install electric lighting seven years before it arrived in Bridport.

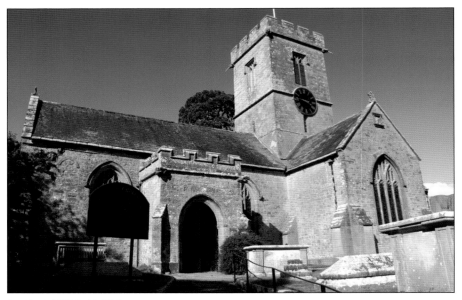

SYMONDSBURY CHURCH

DETAIL OF THE LETHABY STAINED GLASS AT SYMONDSBURY

Today the church has resumed its role as a place of tranquillity and contains three windows of interest. The first and most important is to be seen in the south transept and is a rare example of stained glass by **William Richard Lethaby,** better known as an architect and writer and also a follower of **Pugin, Ruskin** and **Morris.** This highly original interpretation of the *Four Evangelists* is very distinctive due mainly to the expressive faces of the figures; *St Matthew* (on the left) even possesses a passing resemblance to **Ford Madox Brown.** Lethaby may have consulted *Sacred and Legendary Art* an influential book of the time by Mrs. Jameson in order to plan the iconographical aspects of his design. The work dates from 1885 and shows little influence from his contemporaries such as **Morris** or **James Powell & Sons.**

Conveniently a window by the latter can be viewed next on the south side of the chancel. It is in memory of Frederick Webster Maunsell who died in 1914 and clearly it is inspired by late period **Morris & Co.** designs. In some ways it could not be more different to the **Lethaby** glass in its use of dark colours but is still satisfying without being individualistic in any regard.

Lastly the east window provides a chance to see late glass by **C E Kempe & Co. Ltd.** and depicting the *Crucifixion* and the figures of *Mary* and *John.* This dates from 1927 and for such a late date (the firm closed in 1934) its use of canopies and clear glass is anachronistic but oddly convincing.

The architect **E. S. Prior** was married in the church in August 1885.

The church is open most days.

TARRANT GUNVILLE is about six miles to the north-east of Blandford Forum signposted from the A354.

The charming CHURCH OF ST. MARY is found by navigating a lovely path that follows for a while a flint and brick wall that encloses the Old Rectory. The present church dates mainly from an early nineteenth century rebuilding under the architect T.H. Wyatt. Throughout the building are remnants of the previous 1503 church with the lines of the older one being largely followed by its successor.

Inside in the south aisle is a marble tablet to the memory of Thomas Wedgwood, the third son of Josiah Wedgwood forever known as a pioneer in the industrialisation of pottery. Thomas was a pioneer and experimenter in an altogether different field-that of photography. He was also interested in child education and is said to have used the nursery in the near-by manor house as an observation centre.

It is in the chancel however that we encounter decorative murals that bear similarities to the work of **William Morris** and other Victorian designers. They were commissioned in 1910 or thereabouts and there are stencilled decorations in differing colours in the chancel and sanctuary as well as high above the chancel arch. There is a dominant pattern that includes a trifoliate crown and stylized flowers. The work above the chancel arch takes the form of a cross and may be from a later date.

There are texts in Latin high on the three walls of the chancel with further decoration above these some of which is in the form of fleur-de-lys.

The text can be translated as follows:

'Te rogamus audi nos Domine' 'We ask you Lord hear us' (North wall)

'Credo in Sanctam Ecclesiam Catholicain' 'I believe in the Holy Catholic Church' (East wall)

'Ut locum istum et omnes habitantes in eo visitare et consolari digneris' 'So that you might deem this place and all its inhabitants worthy to visit and encourage' (South wall)

The corbels in the shape of angels supporting the roof trusses are also worth noting and typically Victorian.

Finally there is some good stained glass in this church including a nice **C.E. Kempe & Co. Ltd.** east window dating from 1908. It depicts the *Crucifixion* and the saints *Mary* and *John* and has the logo of the company-a wheatsheaf with tower superimposed.

The church is open most days.

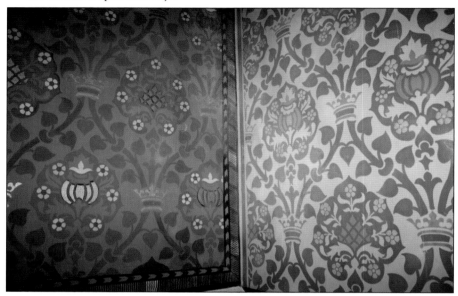

MURALS IN THE CHURCH AT TARRANT GUNVILLE

TARRANT HINTON is found four miles or so from Blandford Forum in a north-easterly direction along the A354.

The CHURCH OF ST. MARY was constructed of flint and sandstone mainly in the fourteenth and fifteenth centuries. Inside on the left-hand side of the chancel (added by Benjamin Ferrey in 1874) is an Easter Sepulchre. This dates from the early sixteenth century and as its name suggests provided the centrepiece for worship at that time of year (it would have had a much deeper recess between the columns originally). Although damaged in places it is still a good example of Renaissance architecture.

The wooden altar rails date from later in the following century but it is the iron and brass lectern close-by that has a definite Art Nouveau style about it. Dating from 1909 it has a gorgeous decorative panel beneath the bookstand that depicts stylised flowers. The rest of the lectern is full of the sinuous line so common to Art Nouveau design. The central panel appears to have the initials AO at the top end and this probably refers to Alpha and Omega-the first and last letters of the Greek alphabet. These letters are often used in stained glass and represent the beginning and end of all things and thus the infinity of God. Alas they do not appear to help identify the maker or designer of such a beautiful piece.

On the west wall of the south aisle is a copy of Hubert and Jan van Eyck's polyptych *The Adoration of the Mystic Lamb* the original of which was consecrated in 1432 for a chapel in St. Bavon's cathedral in Ghent. It was precisely this sort of picture with its new found realism and naturalism in both the portraiture and the landscape that so inspired the Brotherhood early on to attempt to reproduce this style of painting.

In fact **Rossetti** and **Hunt** much admired this picture when they visited St. Bavon's on a trip around Europe in 1849.

The church is occasionally locked but access is possible through the church wardens.

TOLPUDDLE is ten miles north-east of Dorchester off the A35.

The village will forever be linked to the agricultural labourers who in 1834 were sentenced to transportation for establishing a trade union. They did this in order to have a support base from which to negotiate a living wage. The Vicar of Tolpuddle had been involved in negotiations between the six workers and their employers but to no avail. The CHURCH OF ST. JOHN THE EVANGELIST stands near to a seat and shelter with thatched roof commissioned by Ernest Debenham in 1934 to mark the spot

LECTERN AT TARRANT HINTON

where the men are thought to have held their meetings under a large tree. In the north-west corner of the churchyard is a headstone marking the grave of one of the workers who became known as the Tolpuddle Martyrs. It is to the memory of James Hammett who was the only one of the six men to come back to the village to live following his return from Australia.

The Portland headstone with its wreath of chain-links was inscribed and carved by **Eric Gill** and completed in 1934 on the centenary date of their transportation. It was commissioned by the Trades Union Congress as were the Memorial Cottages of the same year to be found at the west end of the village where there is also a later monument.

The church itself was restored by the prolific architect T.H. Wyatt (1807-1880) in 1855 and it is he who is responsible for the pleasing carved corbels with their highly naturalistic vegetation to be seen below the roof supports. The **Minton** tiles also date from this period.

Also in the interior are windows based loosely on **William Holman Hunt's** *The Light of the World* where the painting is now divided into two scenes one entitled *Behold I Stand at the Door and Knock* with the other showing *Christ* with the lantern presumably after being allowed into our hearts and simply called *I Am the Light of the World*.

There is a substantial memorial to the Martyrs outside the Methodist Chapel at the eastern end of Tolpuddle.

The church is open most days.

STAINED GLASS BASED ON "THE LIGHT OF THE WORLD" AT TOLPUDDLE

UPWEY is found four miles north of Weymouth along the Dorchester Road (A354).

The CHURCH OF ST LAURENCE is a large building which was the subject of a 'restoration' in 1891. It was then that the oak pews arrived replacing the previous deal box pews. The church contains two windows from the studios of **Kempe**. The earliest is found in the north aisle and within its three lights shows *St Cecilia*, the *Virgin Mary* and *St Laurence* to whom the church is of course dedicated. It dates from 1894.

Unusually it is overshadowed by the later window completed by **C.E. Kempe & Co. Ltd.** in 1909 and located in the south aisle. A darker window but one with more narrative across its three lights it depicts the *Crucifixion* with the saints *Mary* and *John* watching on as well as other figures that include a centurion.

Also to be seen nearby is a **Minton** tiled pavement in the chancel.

The church is open most days.

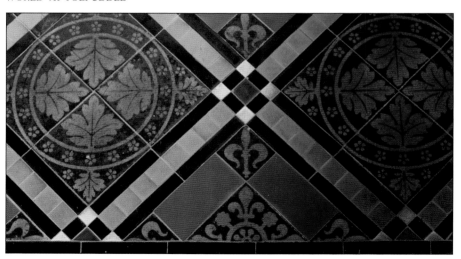

MINTON TILING AT UPWEY

WEST BAY is two miles south of Bridport on the B3157.

The PIER TERRACE (also known previously as Bay House) is found in the centre of the village close to the main car park. The building was previously a hotel and built by **E. S. Prior** in about 1885. It is designed to appear as five terraced houses from either side (the lower one furthest away from the sea is later) although they are not all the same style. The house nearest the sea is deliberately out of rhythm with the other three and although still tile hung it has an additional row of full size windows, whereas the other houses have small dormer windows. The building was the first to be constructed by the West Bay Land and Building Company and unfortunately suffered some fire damage in both 1929 and 1973.

Also in the village are two further buildings by the same architect- Querida and The Moorings. The latter can be found a few yards inland and still in the centre of the village. It is very different in style with a Venetian window and dates from about 1905.

Private houses.

DETAIL OF PRIOR'S BAY HOUSE AT WEST BAY

WEST LULWORTH is a little over eight miles from Wareham in a south-westerly direction on the B3070.

HOLY TRINITY church was built to the designs of the local architect John Hicks and was consecrated in 1870. Its interior contains a number of carvings and

THE MOORINGS BY PRIOR AT WEST BAY

decorative pieces made by craftsmen and women, some local some not, but all completed within the ethos of the Arts and Crafts movement.

The oak reredos is as good a place to start as any with its three panels all enterprisingly painted by Miss Hicks the daughter of the original architect (the building of the church was completed by another local architect C. R. Crickmay following Hicks' death). The two outside panels use the symbolic letters IHS in their design (usually standing for *Iesus Hominum Salvator* or Jesus Saviour of Humankind) whilst the central panel shows a triumphal *Lamb of God* or *Agnes Dei*. Several other local craftsmen were involved in the production of the reredos including the Rev. William Gildea, Basil Sprague and John Chaffey who also helped with the woodwork on the altar, lectern and altar rails as well as other features of the interior. Behind the reredos are panels originating from Oberammergau in Germany and carved by Hans Mayer which depict the *Birth of Christ* and the *Baptism of Christ* with *The Crucifixion* and *Supper at Emmaus* opposite. The church guide suggests that the villagers were inspired to acquire these panels for the church following a lecture at Lulworth in 1894 about the annual Passion Play held in Oberammergau and the carvings also produced in the town. They were installed here a year later.

Yet another local man (Benjamin Grassby) made the wonderful foliage capitals on the columns and the roof corbels.

Another outstanding feature of this church is the stained glass much of it by **Charles Eamer Kempe** or the later **C.E. Kempe & Co. Ltd.** (a moniker used after his death in 1907). They all feature the use of his wheatsheaf signature logo. The best example is undoubtedly the large west window from 1898 with its interpretation of the *Jesse Tree* showing *Jesse* himself in the bottom panel of the second light from the left. Dating from two years later and in the south of the chancel is the three light *Charge to St Peter* whilst

CARVED STONE CAPITAL AT WEST LULWORTH

REREDOS IN WEST LULWORTH CHURCH

on the north side of the church with the wheatsheaf and additional tower logo of work completed after **Kempe's** death there is a window depicting *Christ as the Saviour of the World (Salvador Mundi)* with *St George* and *St Christopher* dating from 1919. There are two other **Kempe** windows of 1900 elsewhere in the church depicting *Christ's* 'appearances' and one by Herbert Bryans who left Kempe's studios in 1897 to run his own business. The window in the south of the nave shows *Christ at Galilee* and dates from 1906.

Of a less Pre-Raphaelite inspiration is the window in the south wall by Arthur Louis Moore (1849-1939) and signed by him. Finally, in this altogether interesting interior there are two memorial plaques probably both by **James Powell & Sons.** They commemorate John Wordsworth, Bishop of Salisbury and a former vicar William Percy Schuster. The former is composed of alabaster and opus sectile and the latter has a lovely decorative alabaster border.

The church is open most days.

As you leave the church glance up the hill in front of you to see **Edwin Lutyens'** house *Weston* of 1927.

Private house.

Also relatively nearby at Lulworth Cove is a Portland headstone with an inscription by **Eric Gill** in memory of Walter Franzen of New York. He fell from the cliff at White Nose in 1927 and died aged thirty-four.

WEST STAFFORD is two and a half miles east of Dorchester via the A352 and Bockhampton Lane.

The CHURCH OF ST ANDREW is another building long associated with the Hardy novel *Tess of the D'Urbevilles* where it appears as Talbothayes church. Within its interior can be found a window by **C.E. Kempe & Co. Ltd.** which features an extraordinary red devil in the lower part of its central light. It dates from 1926, so well after the time of **Kempe's** death and has the logo of the wheatsheaf with a tower superimposed in the lower left hand corner. The subject of this window on the south wall is not surprisingly *Our Lord's Descent into Hades*.

The east window dating from about 1898 also begs attention and may well be by **Christopher Whall** or one of his followers. It forms part of the modifications initiated in memory of Canon Reginald Southwell Smith who was rector for over fifty years and responsible for the reredos and other carvings as well as many of the paintings to be seen adorning woodwork in the church.

The church is open most days.

RED DEVIL DETAIL IN KEMPE GLASS AT WEST STAFFORD

WEYMOUTH is found on the coast nearly nine miles south of Dorchester.

The CHURCH OF ST. MARY is to be found (predictably) in St. Mary Street. Built between 1815-17 by a local man James Hamilton it is made of Portland ashlar and has a neo-classical façade. The church is best known for housing a large painting by James Thornhill of *The Last Supper* dating from 1721. This can be seen immediately one enters the nave positioned as it is above the pilastered reredos with its biblical texts.

However the church also has a number of windows by **James Powell & Sons** at least one of which may be by **Henry Wilson**. These are to be found not in the main body of the church but in the Simeon Room on the south side.

The farthest window from the door shows the biblical scene of the angel at the empty tomb and bears the inscription *He is Risen. He is not here. Behold the place where they laid Him.* The window is dated October 1930 and is in memory of a former church warden. In the left-hand corner it has the 'whitefriar' motif used by **Powells** in later years.

To the right of this window is another depicting a scene of *Jesus with the Fishermen after his Resurrection*. This bold design is a little earlier (1922) and a pleasing composition. Next up is a memorial window to the men of the parish who died in World War I. Here once again the main scene (*St George* in this case) is shown framed by pillars in a superior piece of design.

The final window in this room has the title of *The Hope of the World* and is taken from the painting of the same name by Harold Copping. This was originally completed for the London Missionary Society in 1915 and was very popular in reproduction for many years of the twentieth century. The window also has a date of 1922 but is inscribed with the name of another company that of William Morris of Westminster in the lower right-hand corner. This company had no connection with the man himself but was really attempting to gain success by trading under his name.

Further glass with a Pre-Raphaelite style can be seen in the gallery with two lovely roundels showing details of angel figures either side of the organ pipes. Two other windows nearby of two lights with a roundel over are also in similar style but less appealing.

The church may be locked but access is possible through the church wardens.

The attractive CHURCH OF ST. PAUL is found in Abbotsbury Road in the Westham area of the town. The architect responsible for its design was **George Halford Fellowes Prynne** and it was largely built between 1893-6 with the chancel chapel being added in 1903. St. Paul's was completed during a time when he was successfully building churches for expanding congregations and adapting older buildings. The encaustic tiles in the chancel are contemporary with the construction of the church.

His brother Edward was a painter and designer of stained glass but there is no direct

DETAIL OF JAMES POWELL & SONS GLASS IN ST.MARY'S CHURCH WEYMOUTH

evidence that he worked at St. Paul's. However there is work by him in the collection of the Russell-Cotes Art Gallery and Museum in Bournemouth.

The church may be locked but access is usually possible through the church wardens.

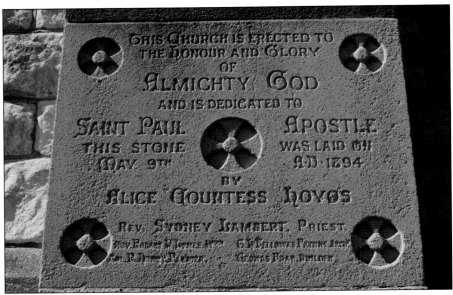

FOUNDATION STONE AT ST. PAUL'S CHURCH WEYMOUTH

The CHURCH OF THE HOLY TRINITY is found to the south of the town bridge in Trinity Road. Although not particularly interesting from the outside, once through its doors the building opens out to form a surprisingly spacious interior. The Gothic styled building was consecrated in 1836 having been designed by Philip Wyatt with a chancel that like most faced east or to the left in this structure. This caused problems in a building such as this because it meant that many members of the congregation would have difficulty seeing the principal aspects of a service or even hearing what was going on. Consequently work started in 1886 (probably by Crickmay & Son) to extend the church and also to reorientate its interior to the present arrangement. We now have two large transepts and a small sanctuary and chancel facing south.

In what is now the Lady Chapel in a large opus sectile reredos by **James Powell & Sons** dating from 1920 and in memory of John Hoppus Devenish and his wife Rosalie. It depicts the *Annunciation* and contains a wonderful level of detail nearby is another pleasing *Annunciation* this time in the form of a low relief sculpture.

The pulpit and font are both made with brown and white veined marble and typical of their time dating from 1905 and 1888 respectively. Also of interest are the angels high up on the organ case and probably carved in Oberammergau, Germany. They were originally on the canopy over the altar but moved to their present position following the installation of the reredos in 1918 as they semi-obscured the *Ascension* window behind.

The reredos in its triptych form is the work of **C.E. Kempe & Co. Ltd.** with the canopy being earlier and later repainted to blend imperceptibly with the reredos.

The church is often open.

INTERIOR OF HOLY TRINITY WEYMOUTH SHOWING KEMPE REREDOS

WIMBORNE is about twelve miles to the north of Poole.

There are two main reasons for visiting THE MINSTER. Firstly there is the striking work of **Thomas Earp** as seen in the carving on the stone pulpit of 1868. At the time this pulpit was completed he was so busy that within five years he would go into partnership with Edwin Hobbs, the firm created later being known as Earp, Son and Hobbs.

Also to be seen in the Minster is the extensive **Minton** encaustic tiling in the choir and sanctuary dating from the time of a restoration by T.H. Wyatt in 1855-7. As well as the tile pavement there is a biblical text on the step in the sanctuary and a tile and mosaic dado.

The Minster is open most days.

POWELL & SONS PANEL IN HOLY TRINITY CHURCH WEYMOUTH

WIMBORNE ST GILES is about ten miles north of Wimborne Minster on the B3078.

The CHURCH OF ST GILES appears here because it was once the home of some

DETAIL OF PULPIT AT WIMBORNE MINSTER

Morris & Co. glass but unfortunately this was lost in a disastrous fire of 1908. The glass was located in an east window and its subject was the *Ascension* to a **Burne-Jones design.** It was completed between 1873-5. After the fire **Sir Ninian Comper** was commissioned to restore the interior and it is known that he adapted a number of windows. He also added the alabaster reredos, font cover, decorated roof and stained glass amidst a rich array of furnishings but it is perhaps his screen which most impresses. This is Gothic in style and very high and extends across the nave and aisles of the church. It all adds up to a colourful and exuberant interior which is not alas to everyone's taste (Nikolaus Pevsner was critical of it) but it is certainly a bold statement by **Comper.** The seventh Earl of Shaftesbury is buried here amongst other family members and there is a memorial in the family pew to this popular figure that improved the working lives of children and founded the Great Ormond Street Hospital in London. A more familiar monument to him is found at Piccadilly Circus where the figure of Eros complete with arrow points towards the village of Wimborne St Giles.

The church is open most days.

WINTERBORNE CAME is about three miles south of Dorchester and signposted from the A352.

To arrive at the CHURCH OF ST. PETER take what appears to be a private drive heading towards Came House, continue through two gates and later a bridleway to the church appears on the right hand side.

The interior of the redundant church contains wonderful stained glass in its west tower window. The design shows figures representing *Faith Hope and Charity* and they are complemented by floral designs with a rich crimson background. The window is by **Henry Holiday** and dates from about 1882. His figure of *Charity* as seen here was used frequently in windows made between the late 1870s and 1890 soon after which he set up his own glass works.

The other glass in the church does not possess the immediate impact on the viewer that the **Holiday** glass has, but is pleasing and signed- J & W Warrington London 1867. The slightly neglected interior also contains a sixteenth century screen with a carved vine and biblical text. Also of interest is a delightful small tablet with a dancing figure within a volute of foliage that is in memory of Mary Frances Seymour Mills who died in 1895 and to whom there is also a worthy gravestone outside the building.

The church is open most days.

DETAIL OF THE FIGURE OF "CHARITY" IN WINTERBORNE CAME CHURCH

WINTERBORNE KINGSTON is seven and a half miles to the south-west of Blandford Forum via the A354.

The CHURCH OF ST. NICHOLAS contains geometric tiles to both sides of the reredos. These were part of **G.E. Street's** restoration of 1872. His work can also be seen in the north aisle and to a lesser extent in the vestry and chancel.

The church is open most days.

WOOTTON FITZPAINE is five miles north-east of Lyme Regis via the A3052, A35 and an unclassified road.

The main reason for visiting is the village hall completed in an Arts and Crafts style. Before getting there however you may pass by the church hidden down a little lane from the road. Whilst the building is very modest and much altered its location is bucolic positioned as it is near Wootton House. Inside the church there is a rather curious window in the south chapel. Although the designer is unknown the east window here has definite affinities with early **Morris** glass which is particularly noticeable in the figures used and in the stylised trees in the background. This feeling is further enhanced by the facial qualities of *Joseph* in the middle panel resembling a young **William Morris.** The dates on the glass make the comparison with early stained glass by **Morris** and his associates even more compelling. However the use of canopies in the composition appears to be inspired by a different source completely. The tiling and mosaic of the Victorian reredos nearby is attractive depicting as it does two angels crouching with scrolls pronouncing Alleluia!

The church is open most days.

The village hall is a further quarter of a mile to the west and was designed by **F. W. Troup** in 1906. The hall is a building of no little sophistication in its use of different materials such as tile, brick lead and wood. **Troup** was particularly keen on using lead and the two commemorative panels are wonderful with their mix of calligraphy and naturalistic detail. The complex vented chimney and main door hinges suggest **Troup's** characteristic involvement with the whole project.

The hall is usually locked when not in use.

MORRISIAN FIGURE IN GLASS AT WOOTTON FITZPAINE CHURCH

THE HALL BY TROUP AT WOOTTON FITZPAINE

LEADWORK DETAIL AT WOOTTON FITZPAINE

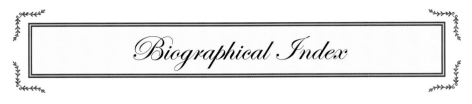

Biographical Index

Charles Robert Ashbee (1863-1942) was a pupil of G.F. Bodley from 1883 and five years later instrumental in the formation of the Guild and School of Handicraft who designed mainly metalwork, jewellery, leatherwork and furniture. In 1901 the Guild moved to Chipping Campden in Gloucestershire a venture that lasted until 1905. Ashbee's silverwork and jewellery designs were much admired and imitated but he also worked in other fields such as interior decoration and ceramics. He set up the Essex House Press in 1896 using materials and equipment from Morris's Kelmscott Press.

Robert Anning Bell (1863-1933) was an artist and designer who studied at the Royal Academy and at one time shared a studio with the sculptor George Frampton and with whom he contributed work for the Arts and Crafts Exhibition Society formed in 1887. He also completed mosaics for the Houses of Parliament and was involved in the design of ceramics at the Della Robbia Pottery in Birkenhead. Anning Bell is also well known for his book designs and illustrations.

William Arthur Smith Benson (1854-1924) chiefly designed metalwork and furniture (he is particularly well known for his lamps and light fittings) both for William Morris and for others but also designed a fair number of buildings. In the early 1880's he established his own business and in 1887 was a founder member of the Art Workers Guild. He also wrote *Elements of Handicraft and Design* in 1893 and after Morris's death in 1896 the company was reformed with Benson as its chairman.

Reginald Theodore Blomfield (1856-1942) was in his early years an architect in harmony with the Arts and Crafts but was increasingly more interested in Classicism during the years 1902-26.

Detmar Blow (1867-1939) was one of the last architects to emulate the work of Ruskin, Webb and Morris. He knew Ruskin as a young man and was present at Morris's funeral. Most of his early work was influenced by the Art and Crafts movement.

George Frederick Bodley (1827-1907) studied under George Gilbert Scott from 1845-50. He then set up his own architectural practice working predominantly in the Gothic Revival style. From 1869-1897 he was in partnership with Thomas Garner. In his early years he was close to the Pre-Raphaelite circle and William Morris in particular.

Henry Thomas Bosdet (1854-1934) studied art at the Royal Academy where he was Curator of the Life School for a number of years and specialised in depicting the nude. Later he was based at Staines and later still had a glass making studio in Chiswick.

John Brett (1831-1902) was an artist whose earlier works were inspired by the teachings of Ruskin. Please see separate chapter in this book for more detailed biographical information.

Eleanor Fortescue Brickdale (1871-1945) was a latter day Pre-Raphaelite painter who also excelled in book illustration and stained glass design. John Byam Shaw was a contemporary and close friend of hers.

Walter Henry Brierley (1862-1926) was an architect influenced by Art and Crafts thinking. One characteristic of his best buildings was his love of detail and use of local materials and style. Typically he encouraged those working with him to develop their crafts and workmanship.

Ford Madox Brown (1821-1893) taught Rossetti briefly in 1848 and through him met other members of the Brotherhood. He joined Morris, Marshall, Faulkner & Co. in 1861 and designed furniture and stained glass for them. His most important paintings are *The Last of England* (1852-55) with its theme of emigration and the social commentary of *Work* (1852-65). His most significant later work can be seen in Manchester Town Hall where he was commissioned to paint a history of the city.

William Burges (1827-1881) was an architect/designer friendly with members of the Pre-Raphaelite Brotherhood who admired their interests in the romantic dream set in a medieval past and which provided the inspiration for his sensational work at Cardiff Castle and Castell Coch.

Edward Coley Burne-Jones (1833-1898) had a few lessons from Rossetti but was largely a self taught artist. He was a close friend of William Morris whom he supplied with many designs for stained glass, tapestry and book illustration as part of Morris & Co. His later painting style was based on that of Botticelli and Michelangelo and other High Renaissance masters.

William Butterfield (1814-1900) established his own architectural practice in 1840. He worked in the Gothic Revival style mainly building churches although he did also produce schools and colleges.

William Douglas Caroe (1857-1938) entered the office of J.L. Pearson in 1881 and four years later was appointed as an architect to the Ecclesiastical Commissioners where he had to prepare plans for many new parish churches. He was a member of the Art Workers' Guild from 1890 and participated enthusiastically in the Arts and Crafts movement.

Richard Cromwell Carpenter (1812-55) was an architect influenced by the Oxford Movement. His designs were therefore allied to High Church principles and included the prominent use of symbolism as seen in Catholic churches. He was a Gothic Revivalist in a relatively restrained manner and for many years was in partnership with William Slater.

Carter & Co. of Poole was a local firm established in 1873 which became very successful making tiles and pottery. They worked in the field of fireplace tiles producing as they did sets of particular subjects such as farmyard scenes and those based on nursery rhymes.

Harry Clarke (1889-1931) was an Irishman who trained under Alfred Child who himself had previously worked with Christopher Whall in London. Clarke's father already headed up a company producing stained glass. When his son was a young man of eighteen he saw the work of such luminaries as Beardsley, Rossetti and Simeon Solomon at an exhibition in Dublin in 1907. He also saw and copied the painting entitled *The Depths of the Sea* by Edward Burne-Jones and altogether the sighting of these works was to have a profound effect on his own artistic development. Six years later Clarke submitted a stained glass design by the name of Unhappy Judas and won the Gold Medal in the Board of Education National Competition in South Kensington. The judges were Walter Crane, Byam Shaw and Selwyn Image and they considered the work to be remarkably original.

Clayton & Bell were one of the largest stained glass studios of the Victorian age. The partners were John Richard Clayton and Alfred Bell and the firm was active from 1855 with the 1860/70s being their busiest time. The company continued to operate until 1993. Their style was influenced by both the Pre-Raphaelites and medieval stained glass.

Benjamin Clemens (1875-1957) was a sculptor who has work in Westminster Abbey and decorative sculpture on the exterior of the Victoria and Albert museum in London.

Hon. John Collier (1850-1934) exhibited at the Royal Academy in 1874-1934. A painter of portraits and upper class life he also produced work with biblical and mythological themes sometimes with a Pre-Raphaelite flavour. He was a pupil of Alma-Tadema and early in his career he received encouragement from Millais.

Ninian Comper (1864-1960) was one of the last Gothic Revival architects. After moving from his native Scotland to London he was articled to C.E. Kempe and later to G.F. Bodley. He was in a partnership with William Bucknall from 1888 until 1905 and is particularly well known for his church furnishings and stained glass designs.

George Edward Cook (1844-1914) is rather an unknown figure although he did exhibit paintings at the Royal Academy in 1872-94.

Walter Crane (1845-1915) was a prolific artist, writer and book illustrator who designed wallpapers, textiles, ceramics and stained glass. As a young man he followed with interest the development of the Pre-Raphaelites and was an admirer of John Ruskin. He later became much involved with the Arts and Crafts movement in particular the Art Workers Guild and the Arts and Crafts Exhibition Society. From the 1880's under the influence of William Morris he worked for the Socialist Party and produced many political cartoons for them.

Thomas Lawrence Dale (1884-1959) was an architect articled to Charles Ponting and a follower of Edwin Lutyens. He also designed a number of churches for the Diocese of Oxford.

Edward Guy Dawber (1862-1938) was a leading Arts and Crafts architect in the Cotswolds based at Bourton-on-the-Hill. He also had a London office and was very successful particularly in the design of country houses.

Evelyn De Morgan (1855-1919) was an artist influenced by her uncle Spencer Stanhope, Burne-Jones and the early Italian masters. She married the potter William De Morgan in 1887.

George Devey (1820-1886) is best known for his skill in designing contemporary buildings in such a way that they used the best aspects of tradition-a central tenet of the Arts and Crafts movement. Both Voysey and Norman Shaw studied under him.

Thomas Earp (1827-93) was a sculptor who worked for such architectural luminaries as Bodley, Street, Teulon and Pugin. Earp's most famous piece of work is probably the Eleanor cross outside of Charing Cross station but he also worked on the Palace of Westminster.

Arthur Romney Green (1872-1945) was a craftsman working mainly in furniture and boat making during the first half of the twentieth century. Inspired by the philosophies and ideas of the Arts and Crafts movement he worked in Haslemere, Surrey and London before setting up in Christchurch in 1920.

Eric Gill (1882-1940) trained with W.D. Caroe and was influenced by the calligrapher Edward Johnston. He was a sculptor, engraver, stonecutter and printmaker. He also designed typeface and is particularly remembered for Gill Sans one of the first modernist designs. He established artist communities in Sussex, Wales and Buckinghamshire.

Ernest Gimson (1864-1919) worked in the office of J.D. Sedding at the recommendation of William Morris. He later met Ernest and Sidney Barnsley and acquired skills in traditional crafts and plasterwork and established a craft community in the Cotswolds. As an architect he built a number of houses and is also noted for his furniture designs.

William Godwin (1813-1883) established a tile company in 1852 with his brother Henry. It moved to larger premises in 1863 producing encaustic and plain geometric tiles.

John Hardman & Co. began stained glass manufacture in 1845 at the suggestion of A.W.N. Pugin who became its chief designer until his death in 1852. His nephew John Hardman Powell then took over and the Birmingham company continue to trade today.

Heaton Butler & Bayne was a popular stained glass firm in Victorian times. Clement Heaton set up a business with James Butler in 1855 the pair being joined in the early 1860's by Robert Turnill Bayne. Their style was mainly Gothic but later designs were inspired by artists such as Rossetti. The company ceased trading in 1953.

Nathaniel Hitch (1845-1938) learnt his trade as an apprentice to the firm of Farmer & Brindley in London who were architectural sculptors working for the likes of Sir Gilbert Scott and Alfred Waterhouse. Later he was employed by another sculptor Thomas Nicholls who completed work for William Burges' Cardiff Castle. This commission from the 3rd. Marquess of Bute transformed the castle into a medieval fantasy inspired by the ideas of the Pre-Raphaelites.

Henry Holiday (1839-1927) was only thirteen when he was taught drawing by William Cave Thomas who had some connections with the Pre-Raphaelite Brotherhood and some of these early works were praised by Ford Madox Brown. In 1855 he started as a student at the Royal Academy and about the same time began a sketching club with Simeon

Solomon and some other artists. Holiday then joined the Artists' Volunteer Corps whose members included Solomon, Morris and Rossetti. In the early 1860's he met and was much influenced by Burne-Jones and following the latter's departure from James Powell & Sons he became a stained glass designer for that firm. He was to spend thirty years there completing many commissions in that time. From 1891 until 1906 he set up his own workshop after which some of his designs were made by Lowndes & Drury. Mary Lowndes was at one time his pupil.

Arthur Hughes (1832-1915) was an artist and illustrator who was arguably the most significant follower of the Pre-Raphaelite Brotherhood with the exception of Madox Brown. After 1870 his technique became much broader but his works were still often faithful to Pre-Raphaelite ideas.

William Holman Hunt (1827-1910) was an artist who formed the Pre-Raphaelite Brotherhood in 1848 with John Everett Millais and Dante Gabriel Rossetti. A great technician he stayed close to the fundamental principles of Pre-Raphaelitism throughout his long career. Please see Introduction for more details.

Owen Jones (1809-1874) was an architect but is best remembered today for his designing, in particular his writings on flat patterning and ornament. He was also an early pioneer in the use of colour lithography which he used when printing a book about the Alhambra in Spain where he visited in 1833 and 1837. His extensive ideas on decoration were further circulated in 1856 with the publication of his magnum opus *The Grammar of Ornament* in which he described his key principles using exquisite illustrations. This book and perhaps a number of Jones' later publications no doubt influenced a young William Morris although his take on what became quite a Victorian fad was almost always an original one.

Charles Eamer Kempe (1837-1907) was a very prolific stained glass designer whose early use of high detail in his compositions gives him a connection to Pre-Raphaelitism. However he probably only had the briefest of contacts with people such as Morris and Burne-Jones although he did know Arthur Hughes quite well.

C.E. Kempe & Co. was the moniker used by the company after C.E. Kempe's death in 1907. The firm continued to operate under his nephew W.E. Tower finally closing in 1934.

William Richard Lethaby (1857-1931) became chief clerk to the architect Richard Norman Shaw from 1879. He joined the Society for the Protection of Buildings (SPAB) where he befriended William Morris and Philip Webb. In 1884 he was co-founder of the Art Workers' Guild and became known not just as an architect but also as a designer of stained glass, furniture and books.

Mary Lowndes (1857-1929) was one of eight children and developed an interest in stained glass design as well as the rights of women. She worked alone to start with but then trained under Henry Holiday when he was chief designer at Powells and whilst there established a friendship with his wife who was also a supporter of the suffrage movement. Lowndes exhibited at a number of art societies and galleries in England between 1884-8. In 1897 she became the co-founder of a stained glass company

Lowndes and Drury in Chelsea conveniently close to the home of Sylvia Pankhurst. This enterprise in collaboration with Alfred Drury became known later as The Glass House and a number of female glass designers and men such as Christopher Whall found work there outside of the commercial constraints of other companies.

Edwin Lutyens (1869-1944) had his own architectural practice from 1888 and during his first building commission met Gertrude Jekyll a garden designer with whom he had a long professional partnership. Initially he designed houses largely in an Arts and Crafts idiom but later produced houses in a more Classical style.

John Everett Millais (1829-1896) founded the Pre-Raphaelite Brotherhood in 1848 with William Holman Hunt and Dante Gabriel Rossetti. His later paintings were criticized by John Ruskin and William Morris and others for their broader paintwork and blander subject matter but these have been re-evaluated more positively by critics in recent years. Please see Introduction for more details.

Herbert Minton (1793-1858) took over his father's earthenware factory and experimented with tile making during the 1830's. By 1845 he was in partnership with Michael Daintry Hollins and they became very successful producing encaustic tiles for churches, institutions and domestic settings. Designers involved with the company included Christopher Dresser, Walter Crane and William Wise.

Arnold Mitchell (1863-1944) worked for a period of time in the offices of Ernest George. He designed a number of schools, village halls and country houses and regularly appeared in the influential periodical The Studio in the early years of the twentieth century. Mitchell developed a large practice of his own and worked extensively in Europe as well as the United Kingdom.

William Morris (1834-1896) was a Victorian polymath being a writer, poet, artist, designer and socialist. He associated with Pre-Raphaelite artists in particular Edward Burne-Jones and was instrumental in forming the ideas of the Arts and Crafts movement. Please see the Introduction for more details of his life.

Morris & Company was the name of the firm reorganised by William Morris in 1875 the forerunner of which was Morris, Marshall, Faulkner & Company set up in 1861.

Noel Laura Nisbet (1887-1956) came from an artistic family in Scotland. After marrying another artist she lived in London where her oils and water-colours were exhibited at the Royal Academy in 1914-38. She specialised in Pre-Raphaelite inspired depictions of fairy tales and allegories usually with large groups of costumed characters.

Karl Parsons (1884-1934) started working in stained glass in 1899 as a pupil of Christopher Whall. He later became his assistant and would have had an apprenticeship steeped in the philosophy of the Arts and Crafts movement. He later had a studio in the Glass House workshops in Fulham founded by Mary Lowndes and A.J. Drury in 1906.

John Loughborough Pearson (1817-1897) was an architect who is most renowned for his creation of superb Gothic spaces- a skill first acquired when building St Augustine's at Kilburn in 1871.

Frederick William Pomeroy (1856-1924) was a member of the Royal Academy and an early sculptor involved with the Art and Crafts movement. He is perhaps best known these days for his large bronze allegorical figures on Vauxhall Bridge in London completed in 1907.

James Powell & Sons were a stained glass company formed when James Powell took over the premises of a seventeenth century glass making concern in 1834. The company continued to produce stained glass until 1973 but their heyday was the latter half of the nineteenth century when they had a number of freelance designers working for them including Edward Burne-Jones. They also made domestic table glassware and opus sectile commemorative panels which are made up of tile pieces of various sizes and were made from the eighteen-sixties until the nineteen-thirties.

Edward Schroeder Prior (1857-1932) was an innovatory architect associated with the Art and Crafts and also a great writer on the subject. In his more mature work he experimented with new materials and strikingly original designs.

George Halford Fellowes Prynne (1853-1927) was previously a pupil of H. Woodyer and an assistant to G.E. Street from 1875. From 1880 he had his own practice. His lesser known brother Edward was a designer of stained glass who was also an artist painting both portraits and genre works occasionally in a Pre-Raphaelite style.

Augustus Welby Northmore Pugin (1812-1852) was a very influential designer and architect of the nineteenth century and an important inspiration and precursor to the Arts and Crafts movement.

Thomas Matthews Rooke (1842-1942) was the studio assistant of Burne–Jones for many years. He also completed a number of paintings with biblical subjects and many architectural ones a practice initiated by Ruskin.

Dante Gabriel Rossetti (1828-1882) was an artist and poet who founded the Pre-Raphaelite Brotherhood with John Everett Millais and William Holman Hunt in 1848. Please see Introduction for more details.

John Ruskin (1819-1900) was the leading art critic of his day and also an accomplished artist in his own right. In 1848 he married Effie Gray but the relationship was never a success with the marriage being annulled in 1854. Effie later married John Everett Millais. Ruskin was a strong supporter of the Pre-Raphaelites during the eighteen-fifties.

Amy Sawyer (active 1887-1909) was an artist influenced by the Art and Crafts movement whose paintings showed an interest in nature and colour harmony. She also produced craft items which incorporated her paintings.

George Gilbert Scott (1811-78) designed mainly ecclesiastical buildings in the Gothic Revival style. He was very prolific and had many pupils including G.F. Bodley and G.E.Street.

George Gilbert Scott Jnr. (1839-97) was an architect and the son of George Gilbert Scott. Although a little overshadowed by other members of this very architectural family he was quite innovatory in his own way.

John Dando Sedding (1838-1891) was an architect best remembered for his Holy Trinity church in Sloane Street, London which has an interior that is the ensemble work of a number of important craftspeople connected to the Arts and Crafts movement. He was a pupil of G.E. Street and later set up office in the capital at 447 Oxford Street next to William Morris. In 1884 he joined the Art Workers Guild with other like minds supportive of the Art and Crafts ideals.

Robert Weir Schultz (1860-1951) moved south to work with Norman Shaw in 1884 and met W.R. Lethaby, Ernest Gimson and the Barnsley brothers as well as other personalities associated with the Arts and Crafts movement. Later he was commissioned by the third Marquess of Bute to design a number of houses in Scotland who was previously responsible for bringing to fulfilment some of William Burges's most extravagant buildings.

John Liston Byam Shaw (1872-1919) was a late Pre-Raphaelite painter, illustrator and occasional designer of stained glass. He exhibited at the Royal Academy from 1893.

Richard Norman Shaw (1831-1912) replaced Philip Webb as G.E. Street's chief draughtsman. Later he had a practice with Eden Nesfield and their mature houses were designed in the Queen Anne style and sometimes finished with interior decoration by Morris & Co. He was one of the most successful architects of the age.

Simeon Solomon (1840-1905) was an artist influenced by Burne-Jones and Rossetti who also worked in book illustration and decorative schemes. His paintings often show aspects of Hebraic history. After his arrest for homosexual offences in 1873 his career lost momentum although he continued to produce many fine drawings with symbolist themes.

John Roddam Spencer Stanhope (1829-1908) was the uncle and teacher of Evelyn De Morgan. He studied under G.F. Watts and was later much inspired by Burne-Jones in his use of mythological and symbolist subjects.

Leonard Stokes (1858-1925) trained in London under such notable Victorian architects as G.E. Street and G.F. Bodley. He designed many churches as well as colleges and houses. He is revered for his work at the Church of St Clare in Liverpool and more curiously was involved in the design of over twenty telephone exchanges (he married the daughter of the General Manager of the National Telephone Company).

George Edmund Street (1824-1881) was a pupil of George Gilbert Scott before setting up his own architectural practice in Oxford in 1852. Amongst his early apprentices were Philip Webb and William Morris. Probably his most well known secular building is the Royal Courts of Justice in London but he also completed many imaginative churches.

Phoebe Traquair (1852-1936) was an illustrator, painter, enameller, bookbinder and embroiderer. Whilst a lot of her mural work is to be found in Scotland (including the song school in St. Mary's cathedral in Edinburgh where amongst the figures depicted there is Rossetti and Holman Hunt) there are examples of her work in other parts of the country.

Francis William Troup (1859-1941) came originally from Aberdeenshire and then worked in Glasgow before setting up his own company in 1891. He became a close friend of another architect and designer Henry Wilson.

Arthur George Walker (1861-1939) was involved in the New Sculpture movement and is perhaps best known for his statue of *Florence Nightingale* in Waterloo Place London but was also responsible for the extraordinary winged figures on the outside of the Church of the Agapemone in Stamford Hill. He exhibited both paintings and sculpture at the Royal Academy from 1884-1937 numbering over eighty pieces. In addition he illustrated books for children up to about 1907. Perhaps his main claim to Pre-Raphaelite fame is that he completed the figure of *William Morris* for the set of thirty-two figures commissioned for the exterior of the V&A museum. He also designed the figure of *Roger Payne* the bookbinder for the same scheme.

Henry Wilson (1864-1934) worked in the practice of J.D. Sedding from 1888 and became his chief assistant. When Sedding suddenly died he took over the business completing some unfinished commissions. Wilson increasingly became more interested in church decoration and is now remembered for his jewellery, silverwork and sculpture. He was president of the Art and Crafts Exhibition Society from 1915-22.

Charles Francis Annesley Voysey (1857-1941) was an architect and designer closely associated with the Arts and Crafts movement. In 1880 he studied for one year under George Devey before setting up his own practice in 1882. As well as architectural work he began to design wallpaper in particular and joined the Art Workers' Guild in 1884. Voysey exhibited both wallpapers and textiles at the first show of the Arts and Crafts Exhibition Society in 1888 and started a long friendship with E.S. Prior from 1894. His country house style is based on vernacular traditions of house building.

Henry Weekes (1807-77) contributed figures to the Albert Memorial in London and to the Oxford University Museum a place brimming with sculptural work associated with the Pre-Raphaelites and where the influence of Ruskin is paramount. Weekes' work in this location has generally been seen to be in a less 'truth to nature' manner than the other sculptures there by Munro, Woolner and Tupper. Weekes was the Professor of Sculpture at the Royal Academy in 1868-76 where he was succeeded by Thomas Woolner.

Philip Speakman Webb (1831-1915) became an assistant to G.E. Street where he met William Morris in 1856. Two years later he set up his own architectural practice with his first commission being Morris's Red House at Bexleyheath. He became a partner in Morris, Marshall, Faulkner & Co. and established the Society for the Protection of Buildings (SPAB) with Morris in 1877. In addition to houses and one church Webb also designed furniture, wallpaper, metalwork and stained glass.

Thomas Woolner (1825-1892) was a member of the original Pre-Raphaelite Brotherhood and with Munro and Tupper one of the main claimants to being an exponent of Pre-Raphaelite sculpture.

Christopher Whall (1849-1924) trained at the Royal Academy but turned to designing stained glass for firms such as Hardman & Co. and James Powell & Sons from 1880. He later set up his own studio in Dorking, Surrey and began to work in conjunction with people like J.D. Sedding, Lethaby and Henry Wilson. In 1897 Mary Lowndes and Alfred Drury helped him to design his windows from London. Later (1906) they established The Glass House in Fulham where he and other glassmakers worked.

Further Reading

Davey, Peter, *Arts and Crafts Architecture,* (Phaidon, London, 1980)

Dobbs, Brian & Judy, *Dante Gabriel Rossetti an Alien Victorian,* (Macdonald and Jane's, London, 1977)

Greensted, Mary, *The Arts and Crafts Movement in Britain,* (Shire, Oxford, 2010)

Harrison, Martin, *Victorian Stained Glass,* (Barrie and Jenkins, London, 1980)

Hilton, Timothy, *The Pre-Raphaelites,* (Thames and Hudson, London, 1970)

Lochnan, Katherine, & Jacobi, Carol (Eds.), *Holman Hunt and the Pre-Raphaelite Vision,* (Art Gallery of Ontario, Toronto, Canada, 2008)

MacCarthy, Fiona, *The Last Pre-Raphaelite: Edward Burne-Jones and the Victorian Imagination,* (Faber and Faber, London, 2011)

Parry, Linda (Ed.), *William Morris,* (Philip Wilson/V&A, London, 1996)

Surtees, Virginia (Ed.), *Sublime & Instructive Letters from John Ruskin to Louisa, Marchioness of Waterford, Anna Blunden and Ellen Heaton,* (Michael Joseph, London 1972)

Payne, Christina, *John Brett: Pre-Raphaelite Landscape Painter,* (Yale University Press, New Haven and London, 2010)

Prettejohn, Elizabeth, *The Art of the Pre-Raphaelites,* (Tate, London, 2000)

Rosenfeld, Jason, & Smith, Alison, *Millais,* (Tate, London, 2007)

Stavridi, Margaret, *Master of Glass: Charles Eamer Kempe 1837-1907,* (John Taylor, Hatfield, 1988)

Treuherz, Julian, *Ford Madox Brown: Pre-Raphaelite Pioneer,* (Philip Wilson, London, 2011)